When Loving *Him* Is Hurting *You*

DR. DAVID HAWKINS

Cover design by Bryce Williamson

Published in association with MacGregor Literary, Inc.

This book includes stories in which people's names and some details of their situations have been changed to protect their privacy.

WHEN LOVING HIM IS HURTING YOU

Published by Harvest House Publishers
Eugene, Oregon 97408
www.harvesthousepublishers.com

ISBN 978-0-7369-6981-9 (pbk.)
ISBN 978-0-7369-6982-6 (eBook)

Library of Congress Cataloging-in-Publication Data

Names: Hawkins, David, 1951- author.
Title: When loving him is hurting you / Dr. David Hawkins.
Description: Eugene Oregon : Harvest House Publishers, [2017]
Identifiers: LCCN 2017001807| ISBN 9780736969819 (pbk.) | ISBN 9780736969826 (eBook)
Subjects: LCSH: Man-woman relationships—Religious aspects—Christianity. | Narcissism—Religious aspects—Christianity. | Men—Psychology. | Marriage—Religious aspects—Christianity. | Interpersonal relations—Religious aspects—Christianity.
Classification: LCC BV4597.53.M36 H39 2017 | DDC 261.8/327—dc23 LC record available at https://lccn.loc.gov/2017001807

Printed in the United States of America

22 23 24 25 / BP-SK / 10 9 8 7

To two beautiful girls who lovingly call me Grampa—Maisie and Kate.

As you enter a world so desperate for change, for equality, and for safety, I envision two strong, vibrant visionaries who can and will speak out and become part of the solution to the problems described in this book.

Contents

INTRODUCTION

W*hen Loving Him Is Hurting You.*

What a title for a book. I so wish the title could have been *When Loving Him Makes Your Heart Sing,* or perhaps *When Loving Him Makes You Smile Wildly.*

That's what love should be about, after all. Loving him should be so self-evident that people in the grocery line stop and ask, "Why are you smiling?" and you respond, "Because I love my husband so much and he loves me just as much in return."

That's what love is about, isn't it?

We know a lot about healthy love. We know in healthy love we feel larger, stronger, safer than when we are alone. We feel bold and secure, able to move about in the world with confidence because we are deeply and securely loved.

You are likely reading this book because you have felt deeply disappointed in love. Rather than smiling wildly, you feel discouraged and fearful. You have lost much of your hopefulness and seek ways to regain it.

You will find that hope in this book and in the friends you will meet here. You will find help and encouragement in these pages. Amid the stories of women like you, you'll find advice on how to not only survive your situation but also thrive once again. In addition to hope, you will find healing.

I admit that as I prepared to write this book, I wondered if I could do the topic justice. How could I possibly give voice to the thousands of women I've counseled over the past ten years as I've spent countless hours with victims and perpetrators of narcissistic and emotional abuse? How could I possibly put into words the depth of their fears and anxieties? Narcissistic and emotional abuse is, after all, incredibly elusive. Often hard to define, emotional abuse is experienced more than recognized.

You, more than many others, know about the elusive aspect of this problem. You know the countless people you've reached out to for support and help, only to feel abandoned and discounted. In asking for help, you've received platitudes and shallow words of counsel. You've received even worse—dismissive comments—when suffering from a broken heart, a troubled mind, and a hurting body.

You will find an understanding voice in this book, albeit inadequate, for no one can possibly know what you are experiencing except those who have walked your journey. Nonetheless, in these pages you will find stories and counsel to meet you at your places of pain.

As I've written, I've been aware of so much more that is needed. Another book is needed as a follow-up to this one and then perhaps another after that. We are on the cutting edge of knowledge about the debilitating phenomenon called narcissistic and emotional abuse.

My writing and speaking on this topic have left me feeling a bit discouraged. I fear we have set our sights far too low. I fear we have settled for love that isn't love. We have settled for a kind of love that reflects tolerance or worse, harm. We—your pastors, counselors, friends, and family—have sold you something you should no longer buy. Love, to be love, must leave you heartened and happy, not hurting and discouraged.

When Loving Him Is Hurting You, as you may sense, was not easy to write. It has not been easy to sit with thousands—yes, thousands—of women who have argued to be heard, and rightfully so. Having been dismissed and discounted, blamed and shamed, their voices have been all but silenced. They have shared their stories of narcissistic and emotional abuse, stories they have mostly kept silent for fear of feeling further shame and misunderstanding. It has been an impossible journey you know all too well.

The victims of abuse have entrusted me with their stories, and I have the responsibility to retell them accurately and to offer hope for those still searching for answers to their pain. It is time for things to change. It is time we listened to their stories, heard the truths in them, and made drastic changes. We will share friendship, compassion, stories, and solutions in this book.

I wish we were beyond men using women to support their vulnerable egos. I so wish we were beyond patriarchal communities, churches, societies, and nations where women are harmed physically, emotionally, and spiritually. While we seem to have made inroads into physical domestic violence, we have only begun to wage war against narcissistic and emotional abuse. Join me on this path of recovery, which begins with understanding and leads to speaking out and setting boundaries against it.

It is strange to live in such an uneducated, uninformed, and harmful world, where emotional abuse—considered by many to be even more damaging than physical violence—is allowed to run amok. This horrific form of violence is everywhere, yet interventions are unheard of. This must stop.

I have the honor to peer into this dark world and shine the tiniest bit of light. It is dark because abused women still feel stigmatized about speaking out against it. It is dark because we don't want to admit this kind of abuse exists, much like slavery of years ago and sex trafficking today. We are so ashamed of this covert abuse that we simply refuse to talk about it. Again, this must stop.

I share in this book that we really do know, in ways we cannot openly admit, about this abuse. We can't help but know about it since it exists *everywhere*. You cannot ride a bus, train, or plane without seeing someone cower in fear. You cannot gather with your extended family without seeing and hearing about this abuse. Yet we turn away. It is still too frightening to speak out when you know you will be dismissed. You cannot go out in public and not hear a man yell obscenities at a woman, and yet we numb ourselves to it. You are part of a group of people speaking boldly that this must stop.

There is, thankfully, a new wind blowing. There are strong female voices, perhaps some of the same ones who have spoken out about physical domestic violence, who recognize emotional violence is just as harmful and must be stopped. Young and old, women are standing up and speaking about the unspeakable debilitating impact of narcissistic and emotional abuse. This familiar, everyday form of violence is finally receiving press. People are finally beginning to listen. Women with daily migraine headaches, adrenal failure, anxiety, and depression are finding the strength to say this form of violence must stop. You are part of this healing community. Welcome.

I am pleased you are reading this book. You are part of a growing, strong, influential group of women (and men) who will speak out against abuse in all forms. Let's keep the conversation going. I will keep writing, counseling, speaking, and learning. Will you join me?

Part 1

Narcissism

1

Swept Off Your Feet

Do not think of yourself more highly than you ought.

ROMANS 12:3

I don't know what happened," Susan told me, rubbing her temples to ease the physical pain from her lingering emotional struggles.

Susan, a warm and sensitive 46-year-old divorced mother of two adolescent girls, had reentered the dating scene with some trepidation and more than a dash of caution.

"He was such a smooth talker," she continued. "He was so caring, kind, and wonderful. He was a strong Christian leader, active in the singles ministry at our church. I should have known something was wrong when I thought this was too good to be true. It was too good to be true."

Susan had first met Jeff, a bold and daring Realtor, at their church. He was also divorced and dating. Both had proclaimed caution regarding dating, though attraction overwhelmed their best intentions to "go slow." This would be no slow romance. In fact, he proposed to her after only three months of dating.

"I knew it was too soon," she admitted, still holding her head, "but we wanted to be celibate until married, and everything seemed so right. I feel like such a fool now."

Chemistry certainly has a way of clouding our thoughts and best intentions. However, to be fair to Susan, anyone can be swept off her feet, especially if the one doing the sweeping is daring, talented, and good-looking. Being a great talker and a good listener with a wit that had no limits, Jeff's dating resume was strong.

Jeff is not a bad guy. Far from it. He is liked by many. He has a cadre of friends, is active in the chamber of commerce, teaches classes at his church, and is financially stable. He has three children who truly care about him. He is not a diabolical, scheming Cassanova. Jeff is, however, dangerous.

Susan was swept off her feet by Jeff's wonderful traits. They are real, and she is not the first person to have been swept up in his charisma. Jeff is bright, charming...and narcissistic, and that is enough to cause serious trouble for any woman. Now, three years into their marriage, she is desperately trying to regain her emotional footing and recover her life.

If you, like Susan, have met a narcissistic man and are spinning from love gone wrong, keep reading.

Narcissus

The problem of narcissism is not new. The term "narcissism" comes from Greek mythology. Narcissus was a hunter, renowned for his beauty. He was exceptionally proud and handsome, and he knew it. His enemy, Nemesis, discovered his weakness and devised a plan to use it. Nemesis lured Narcissus to a pool where Narcissus fell in love with his own reflection in the water. Unable to pull himself away, Narcissus fell under the spell of his own image and drowned.

The story of Narcissus is far from an old, irrelevant myth—it is the basis of a severe character issue that is devastating to those involved. The truths of this dark drama have survived throughout the centuries. Shallow self-adoration (narcissism) is at the root of many serious disorders. Far from being a simple and benign problem, narcissism wreaks havoc not only in the one who has those traits but also with all who are unwittingly ensnared in relationships with him. Self-obsession leads to death of the self as well as death of the relationship.

The myth of Narcissus and the truths it warns against must inform us today. We must learn more about the dangers of self-love and self-centeredness and their devastating impact if we are going to have healthy relationships. We must learn what Scripture has to say about self-love and the influence it has on our ability to relate effectively in the world.

You and Narcissism

Many seem to be talking about narcissism, and everyone seems to be an expert. Everyone is quick to offer counsel on what to do with your narcissistic man, sure that they know what is right for your life. You know, however, that nothing is that simple. You know your relationship with your man is complex, and your questions have no simple answers. If we begin to understand more about this problem, we can move into what you can do to make healthier choices.

You're likely reading this book because you've been on the emotional roller coaster with someone with narcissistic traits. Like Susan, you may have believed your situation was too good to be true and discovered your worst fears were correct. Originally believing it was your good fortune to find someone who was charming, intelligent, determined, and decisive, now you're not so sure.

It started so well. You were captivated by his attention, enamored with his charm, engulfed in his persistence to have a relationship with you. But the thorns quickly began to grow on the rose. Blue skies became cloudy. As you brought your concerns to him, he rebutted with excuses. Every problem of yours came with excuses from him. His defensiveness, rationalizations, and blame shifting from him have left your head spinning. You are confused and wondering what hit you.

Narcissism has suddenly become more than an old myth, a story of a self-centered young man. For you it is real, powerful, and incredibly disconcerting. Are you considering leaving the relationship? Are you ambivalent? You feel confused. You care about him. His good traits are still good. You have invested time, energy, and love, and things are not as simple as some might imagine. No one simply walks away when trouble emerges, right? With mixed feelings come jangled thoughts, and with jangled thoughts come more confusion.

The problem now isn't just that you have mixed feelings. Everyone has mixed feelings about nearly everything. You can deal with that. Your situation is now more serious. When you recoil at his self-centered actions, he blames you and tells you you're wrong. You become more confused. You complain when he rationalizes his childish behavior, only to be told you're the one who's behaving badly. The comingling of positive and negative interactions has you reeling.

It is natural to seek relief from the very person causing you harm, yet to do so brings even more problems. Just as quickly as you complain to him, he reverses the blame onto you! In fact, he ups the ante, firing myriad criticisms at you, causing you to wonder what is going on.

"You will never be satisfied," he says.

"You blame me for everything," he challenges.

"You care about everyone more than me," he yells.

"I give and give to you and get nothing in return," he insults.

He says he loves you, but he is never satisfied. You are left with your head spinning. Does he love you or not? If only the question were that simple. It is not!

What are you to do with a relationship like this? When it's good, it's very good, and when it's bad, it's very bad. What about a relationship where you are treated like a queen one day and the archenemy the next? How do you make sense out of something that simply does not make sense? It's not so easy to make quick decisions here.

This book is about relating to a narcissistic man—a man who is so very charming, very delightful, very persuasive. It's about getting your bearings so your head will stop spinning and you can see which way is up. It's about stepping back, learning all you can about narcissism, and then making good decisions about the future of your relationship.

Love at First Sight

Many don't believe in love at first sight. Don't say that to Ginny, a 34-year-old woman who came to see me at the Marriage Recovery Center with her husband, Danny.

Married for six years, both said their marriage was a dream for the first couple of years. I asked them to give me a history of their problems and why they were reaching out for help.

"He was so delightful," Ginny enthused. She leaned back in her chair, brushed her blonde hair out of her face, and smiled brightly as she recalled their early years.

"I waited until my late twenties to get married. He swept me off my feet. He was everything I was looking for in a man. He took time listening to me. He was considerate, kind, and attentive. I absolutely fell for him."

She paused and reflected, glancing over at her husband, who stared blankly at her.

"I had dated some other guys who weren't nearly as attentive as Danny. They were self-centered and shallow. He was caring and asked me lots of questions. He really seemed to care."

"What went wrong?" I asked. Danny sat motionless as he listened to Ginny tell her story. He seemed unmoved by her pain.

"Then it became all about him," she said with obvious sadness. She began to cry, though he still sat distant and apparently unempathetic.

"I worked while he went to law school," she continued. "I kept working while he built his practice, even though we had two girls in the first few years of marriage. He rarely asked about my life and my world, focusing his attention on his practice and his status in the community. He joined every civic group he could to build his reputation—and it worked. But I got lost. I don't know if he even knows how I spend my days."

Danny frowned as Ginny continued to share with me.

"I don't see it that way at all," he said finally with disdain. "I worked my tail off in law school and now work 60 hours a week so she can have a big house and a nice car. I can't believe I'm not getting more respect. Her tears just make me sick. I'm the one almost killing myself for everyone, and this is what I get for it?"

"See what I mean?" Ginny asked. "I share my pain, and his is always bigger. He has it worse than anyone, hurts more than anyone, and can't hear about my feelings. I feel absolutely alone in this marriage."

"I feel just as alone, Ginny," Danny shouted derisively. "Don't you get that? I feel just as alone. You're not the only one hurting here." Danny jumped up and began pacing the room, giving periodic angry glances to me and his wife.

Such was the beginning of their counseling process. While both were hurting—typical of marriages coming to my Marriage Recovery Center—Danny's wounds always seemed to be bigger than Ginny's. His point of view always took precedence over her perspective. Her desires took second place to his. My work was cut out for me.

The Sin of Narcissism

The central issue here is not just that narcissism causes problems in a relationship. Narcissism does that and far more! The central issue is not that narcissism is an imbalance within the personality. The central issue is that narcissism is also sin.

Yes, those are strong words. We are more comfortable calling narcissism a character defect or a thinking error. We are quick to label someone a narcissist or a man who has narcissistic traits. Certainly it is those things as well as a diagnosable problem. But it is also sin.

How can I make such a brazen claim? Reflect for a moment with me on these words from the apostle Paul:

> For by the grace given me I say to every one of you: Do not think of yourself more highly than you ought, but rather think of yourself with sober judgment, in accordance with the faith God has distributed to each of you (Romans 12:3).

These words are piercing and make clear how we as Christians ought to conduct ourselves. Narcissism is out! Humility is in!

Solomon, the wisest man who has ever lived, said this about the narcissist:

> The proud and the arrogant person—"Mocker" is his name—behaves with insolent fury (Proverbs 21:24).

He goes on to say we must avoid such a person!

Finally, Jesus had this to say about how we should conduct ourselves:

> Whoever wants to become great among you must be your servant, and whoever wants to be first must be slave of all. For

> even the Son of Man did not come to be served, but to serve, and to give his life as a ransom for many (Mark 10:43-45).

These are but a few of the Scriptures indicting arrogance. Yet it is so easy to puff ourselves up and put others down. There is a bit of the mocker in all of us.

Consider the ways you may think of yourself as slightly above others. Narcissism is not only damaging and hurtful, it is sinful and must not be ignored or enabled.

Traits of Narcissistic Personality Disorder

Unfortunately, most of us aren't sure where self-centeredness ends and narcissism begins. Furthermore, we're not sure whether someone has a diagnosable problem or is simply pompous.

To add to the problem, there is conflicting information on the Internet and in books about narcissism. The flood of broken and damaged relationships has led some people to label any self-centeredness as narcissism. Someone told me recently they thought narcissism was the diagnosis du jour.

Narcissistic personality disorder (NPD) seems to be the latest diagnosis in vogue. For the longest time we were diagnosing kids and then adults with attention deficit disorder. Then came borderline personality disorder. Now we have narcissistic personality disorder.

Anytime we're annoyed with our mate, anytime they get into a mood or push their agenda, we're tempted to scream, "Narcissist!" Sometimes the label fits—sometimes not. Let's see if this helps determine the difference.

The American Psychiatric Association's Diagnostic and Statistical Manual of Mental Disorders lists these symptoms as necessary to legitimately render a diagnosis of NPD. You must have at least five of the following criteria to fit the diagnosis:

- Exhibits an exaggerated sense of self-importance
- Has a preoccupation with fantasies of unlimited success, power, brilliance, beauty, or ideal love

- Believes he is "special" and can only be understood by, or should associate with, other special or high-status people
- Requires excessive admiration
- Has a sense of entitlement
- Selfishly takes advantage of others to achieve his own ends
- Lacks empathy
- Is often envious of others or believes that others are envious of him
- Shows arrogant, haughty, patronizing, or contemptuous behaviors or attitudes

In addition to these criteria for a diagnosis of NPD, the APA states,

> If NPD is caused by infantile damage and consequent developmental short-circuits, it probably represents an irremediable condition. However, if narcissism is a behavior pattern that's learned, then there is some hope, however tenuous, that it's a behavior pattern that can be unlearned.[1]

It's time to become more active, and I will help you separate facts from fiction, feelings from fantasy. Together we will look at the facts and consider the possibilities so you can choose your future wisely.

The Headlines on Narcissism

Narcissists have received a lot of negative press—much of it deserved. Narcissism is devastating. However, many of the headlines on narcissism only create more confusion. You've probably read things like these:

- "They'll never change."
- "You're going to get caught in their snare and get trapped."
- "They reel you in and fling you out."

- "You'll leave in much worse shape than when you started."
- "Once a narcissist, always a narcissist."
- "Your self-esteem will never be the same."

Oh my! Is this all true? Is it really that disastrous? Is it true that it's absolutely dire if your mate has narcissistic traits? If you have narcissistic traits, then do you have NPD? If he has narcissistic traits, should you run?

These are all great questions. I'm alarmed, however, at the blogs announcing the end to your sanity if you have a relationship with someone with narcissistic traits.

Now, before you throw this book against the wall in disgust, please understand that I've worked with hundreds of men with narcissistic traits. This book will look at narcissistic men from every possible angle, and you will learn the truth about narcissism and your best response to it.

Narcissistic Traits

As we have discussed, not every man with narcissistic traits has NPD. As with most personality disorders, this is best understood as a spectrum on which your man may fall. Narcissism is best understood *not* as an all-or-nothing phenomenon, but rather a low-to-high continuum.

My client, Danny, is likely to have narcissistic traits but not full-blown NPD. To a misunderstanding eye, he may appear to have NPD. A reading of the traits for NPD may yield "yes, yes, yes, yes, and yes." Again, let's consider the phenomenon of narcissism as being on a spectrum, from low to high.

Is Danny self-centered? Quite likely! Is he powerful, and does he push his own agenda? Yes. Does he lack deep, endearing empathy for his wife? Again, yes. Does he act entitled? Sometimes. Is he preoccupied with fantasies of unlimited power, success, and beauty? Maybe. Does he take advantage of others to meet his own needs? Not often. Is he willing to seek help and possibly change? The jury is still out!

So you see, the picture can be a bit more muddled than we originally thought. This is what I often face—a mixed picture with uncertain outcomes. I've counseled hundreds of men who clearly had narcissistic traits, but the majority did *not* have NPD. Rather, they had traits that needed attention and intervention.

It is possible that you are involved with a man who, like Danny, has some narcissistic traits. As we get deeper into the book, we will explore what to do if your man has mild narcissistic traits, moderate traits, or full-blown NPD, and you'll learn how to recognize the difference. We will address what to do in each situation.

A Little Narcissism Is Too Much

Just as I offer guarded hope for the mate of a narcissist, I must also emphasize that a little narcissism goes a long way. A little bit of crazy making is enough to make your head spin. In no way am I suggesting that narcissism is just another problem that can be easily remedied.

Think about it. Let's take just one trait of the narcissist and consider the impact. For example, consider the lack of empathy.

You come home from a tough day at the office and want to talk about it with your man. You're not looking to complain all evening. You simply want to share about your rough day. You begin talking about someone at work, and your man shrugs, giving you quick advice.

"You shouldn't put up with that," he states.

"I have to put up with it," you say, getting defensive. "It's part of my job."

"You need to tell your boss it's intolerable," he says. "That's what I'd do. I wouldn't take it."

"You're not understanding," you say, trying to explain. "I just wanted to vent a little about my day."

"Well, all you do is complain," he says unsympathetically.

You walk away, feeling unheard, uncared for, and alone. No empathy. No compassion. You're left wondering if you have done something wrong.

It's a small thing, really—not enough to break a marriage. But day in and day out, it takes a toll on you. A little bit of narcissism is devastating.

Dr. Jekyll and Mr. Hyde

My intent is not to quibble over whether your man is a bona fide narcissist. It's about identifying the traits that make up narcissism and learning what you can do if your mate has narcissistic traits and how you can make healthy choices about it.

In all aspects of life, we must step back from a situation or relationship and make a judgment. Is this relationship healthy for me? Can I be myself in this relationship, or does coping within the relationship cost too much? Do the cons outweigh the pros in this relationship?

One of the descriptors often used by women in describing their man is "Dr. Jekyll and Mr. Hyde," aptly named after the character with the alter ego. In that story by Robert Louis Stevenson, we are faced with the dual nature of a man. Dr. Jekyll has a dark side—Mr. Hyde. One side is angelic, but the other side is devilish.

The novel contains striking contrasts in characters, but there is a certain truth about the novel in all of us and certainly within the narcissistic man. Many men have the good qualities of Dr. Jekyll, and this part of a man's character can be quite charming and even mesmerizing. However, within the narcissistic man is also Mr. Hyde—quite capable of being self-centered, shallow, and hurtful.

Staying Alive

You're reading this book because you have fallen in love with the caring aspect of your man—Dr. Jekyll. You were infatuated by his charm and seduced by his wit and admiration, and you became enmeshed with him.

Over time you came to see the darker side of his personality—Mr. Hyde. You've discovered how easily he can be hurt. When hurt, he turns on you and blames you for his problems. With your head spinning, you think about getting out of the relationship but also discover that he needs you. In fact, you both need each other.

As you move forward, your needs must change. You must become more familiar with his character, learning why you became attached to him, why you have stayed, and what you will do in the future. It's time to step back and reflect on your man. This will not be an easy task, but it is one you can do. It is not likely, however, that you will obtain a perfectly clear picture. Life is rarely that black and white. However, as you understand him more, you can learn to trust yourself again. You can determine what traits in him need to be changed and how you can set boundaries—either he makes those necessary changes or you leave the relationship. Either way, you will discover a way to be healthy.

Consider that this relationship is an opportunity for you to grow. In this book you will have many opportunities to discern how you can grow and even thrive. By answering tough questions and being honest with yourself, you will gain clarity and discover the direction to take.

The Path Forward

I can assure you that as you read this book, you will understand narcissism better. And more important, you will know how to proceed. You will discern either how to recover from your narcissistic relationship or how to create an intervention to determine whether your narcissistic man can and will change. You will learn how...

- The narcissist uses personality to gain power.
- You may be prone to falling in love with a narcissist.
- Narcissists are thin-skinned and easily hurt, and the impact that has on you.
- Narcissists are wounded little boys inside.
- You lose your life to the narcissist.
- You can begin to change the dynamics of the narcissistic relationship.
- You can rediscover and recover your life.

- You can use boundaries effectively with narcissists.
- God will help you develop clarity and be with you on your path of healing.

Your life is not over simply because you may be involved with a narcissist. Whatever your relationship with a narcissist, let's journey together with God as our guide.

2

Power, Privilege, and Personality

Once God has spoken; twice have I heard this: that power belongs to God.

PSALM 62:11 NASB

Narcissism and emotional abuse are all about power. Add privilege and personality, and boom, you have a one-two-three punch. It is critical that you learn about that power, how it might impact you, and how you can learn to make healthy choices based on this new knowledge.

Think about it. Narcissists are consummate egomaniacs, ready to take over every situation. Even if they start out soft and deferent, they quickly exert their influence. They overwhelm others with the sheer force of their personality, and therefore you must learn about the power tactics of narcissists. This is what this chapter is about.

When I reflect on this one-two-three punch—power, privilege, and personality—I quiver. I'm no lightweight, and yet when I face a man who thinks he's indomitable, I'm temporarily stupefied. I'm not sure about myself—what I think, want, or need. No wonder countless women get caught in relationships with powerful men and then feel powerless to escape.

I just wrapped up a marriage intensive that did not go well, and there was one reason our time and progress was compromised: a very powerful, intimidating, and smug man. He came in puffing out his chest and left with much the same attitude.

I had a sinking feeling at the first hello. His handshake was firm, and I could tell by the look in his eyes that his hello really meant, "I don't want to be here. You better side with me, or I'm leaving."

"This is my last effort," he added. "I'm not here because I want to be. She fires anyone who doesn't go along with her. We'll see how this goes. If this doesn't work, I'm out of here."

Okay, not the warmest greeting! There was no "I'm so thankful to be here," which is typical. There was no "I'm ready to change and invite you to point out what I might be doing to help create the problems we have."

No. Just a marking of his territory. I was put on notice and scrambled, deciding how I would respond to him.

When dealing with narcissists, such an initial greeting is not remarkable. They don't typically come knocking on my door looking for help. Generally lacking insight and resistant to change, they come because their mate has given them an ultimatum. While necessary to get them to my door, such circumstances don't often do much to endear them to me. My work was, once again, cut out for me.

Adam and Every Woman

This man was not completely unusual. Posturing and strutting are two of the power tactics used by the narcissist and emotionally abusive man. Learning how to deal effectively with emotionally abusive men has become a customary part of my practice. I had to learn about power, and now I will teach you.

Many powerful men create havoc by their forcefulness. Strong, determined, and bullheaded, they can be overwhelming. But this is not a new syndrome. The push for power started long ago. Let's start there.

We can hardly blame them. Adam and Eve were just like us. They enjoyed all the comforts lavished on them, and then, when given the opportunity to add power to the mix, the temptation was simply too great.

There they were, in the Garden of Eden, where their every desire was met. They could walk freely in the garden and eat from any of the trees except one. "The LORD God warned him, 'You may freely eat the fruit of every tree in the garden—except the tree of the knowledge of good and evil. If you eat its fruit, you are sure to die'" (Genesis 2:16-17 NLT).

It initially appeared that our wonderful beginning would have a happy ending. Satan, however, in the form of a serpent, taunted Eve with the promise of power.

"'You will not certainly die,' the serpent said to the woman. 'For God knows that when you eat from it your eyes will be opened, and you will be like God, knowing good and evil'" (Genesis 3:4-5).

And so Adam and Eve decided they wanted to be wise and powerful like God, and our lives were forever changed.

Just like Adam and Eve

I'd like to believe I would have withstood the serpent's taunting to obtain power, but deep down I know it's not true. I cannot limit my indulgence in a buffet line, stop myself from overworking, inhibit my overspending, or control any number of other vices. I cannot withstand the temptation to buy a nicer car than my neighbor, let alone stand up against the possibility of having the power of God. Who am I trying to kid?

This is not to say we are all narcissistic or emotionally abusive. We're not! I take some comfort in knowing I am just like everyone and, in fact, just like Adam and Eve. We are all susceptible and vulnerable to the lure of power, prestige, and personality.

Notice the incredible draw of the Kardashians, the stars on *Dancing with the Stars*, or your favorite celebrity. Notice how we have an insatiable desire to learn about the glittering people and secretly wish we could have just a bit of their glitter ourselves. Understand that it is not just the glitter that tempts us, but the power that glitter buys. These stars can have anything they want!

The narcissist drinks from that same well. He wants that power and admiration and believes he is that star!

For all that star power, however, most of us know when to put on the brakes. Overspending is one thing; taking advantage of and exploiting others for our own gain is something quite different. Lusting after your colleague's recent vacation to the Bahamas is one thing; stubbornly refusing to listen to your mate's pleas for attention and care and neglecting her is something else.

Privilege and Personality

We should not be surprised that stars enjoy a certain heightened power, given their money, fame, and status in our culture. Celebrities are, well, celebrated. We pay them extraordinarily well and give them endless privileges. Combine this privileged status with personality, and they have power.

Power has always had the possibility of corrupting. Power—the ability to make choices others cannot make, to do things others cannot do—can be intoxicating and changes people.

We expect stars to act with a certain arrogance. What is it about others that makes them narcissistic? Are there certain people prone to thinking they are better than others? The answer to that is, quite obviously, yes. At least there are those who *believe* they are better than the rest of us. You have seen them. You know you are around people who believe they are special, a cut above, by the way they carry themselves and the way they talk to the rest of us.

Just the other day my wife and I went into an expensive, boutique design store and expected to be treated well by the clerk. We weren't treated well at all. After being ignored for a few minutes, we finally got his attention. Treated stiffly, we shopped for a few moments and then left. I felt uneasy as we left the store.

At the moment I couldn't discern why I felt uneasy—*less than.*

Upon leaving the store, Christie commented, "Did you feel like we just had a *Pretty Woman* moment?"

"Huh?" I asked.

"You know, when Julia Roberts goes shopping in *Pretty Woman* and the lady in the store tells her she can't afford to shop there. I felt like that in there."

"Maybe so," I said.

"That is a specialty store," Christie added. "It caters to a lot of high-end clients, and the clerk is probably used to selling to privileged people. Maybe he figured we weren't going to buy anything, so why waste time on us. I don't know. He was sure rude though."

There it was—being treated poorly. Being talked to in a condescending way so as to establish the pecking order. This clerk, simply by the way he carried himself and the way he treated us, made us feel "less than." He let us know by his actions that the store was above us.

If Christie and I felt "less than" in this simple setting, imagine multiplying this experience in a marriage with a power differential. Imagine a woman with less power functioning day in and day out with a man who exerts his influence. Personality plus privilege packs a powerful punch.

Backstage

I often wonder what we would see if we were offered a peek backstage with celebrities. With lights and camera off and pretenses set aside, we often see another side to people's personalities. What might we see behind the scenes?

I suggest we would often see an abundance of power tactics. We could possibly witness times of intimidation, forcefulness, and an insistence on their way. We might see tempers flare in the face of frustration. Rarely do people rise to levels of influence with passivity.

Without exception, the many narcissists I've treated have had dominance in their personality that is formidable. Charismatic and personable, they are pleasant as long as things go their way. When met with frustration, they can be bulldozers. They know what they want, and their charm and pleasantries may give way to something quite different if barriers are put in their path.

In my book *Dealing with the CrazyMakers in Your Life*, I note that aggressors and narcissists are likely to intimidate, threaten, and throw temper tantrums to get you to go along with their schemes. They paralyze us with their intensity, causing us to shrink back and go along with whatever they want.

Knowing this can be a power equalizer. Preparing for their use of power can be a way to mitigate some of that power. We will learn more about this further along in the book.

Entitled Privilege

Entitlement is one of the hallmark traits of the narcissist. As if power and personality were not enough, now he believes these grant him special privileges. We can feel his entitlement in the way he moves, the way he talks, and the way he expects others to treat him. He's special.

Power, gained either through money, political status, or personality—sometimes an aggressive personality—is, in its purest form, the ability to influence others. These common attributes of power open doors, gain additional privileges, and then change the brains of those who wield power.

Power hungry and power fed, powerful people often act entitled. They may dominate and even intimidate—more power tactics. We feel domination. We sense intimidation and must be wary of it. We must recognize it in colleagues, bosses, friends, and of course, mates.

I worked with a man named Jake who exemplified this issue. Jake rose up quickly in his law firm, starting out as an intern and becoming a partner in just ten years. He had the advantage of a good background.

The son of two powerful businesspeople in a large East Coast city, Jake was destined for power. He already had privilege and personality, and power often follows. He was an only child, and his parents expected greatness. He attended private schools and then an Ivy League university. His trajectory was set at an early age. He lived a life of privilege and learned to use the power it garnered him. His college was selected for him, and he was given two choices for career: law or medicine. He chose law.

Jake's scholastic achievements and performance in the law firm, combined with a few parental connections, expedited his rise in rank, power, and privilege. His parents endowed him with a college education and healthy bank account and paid for his country club membership.

With few obstacles in his path, he developed a gregarious personality. His early adulthood continued smoothly. He married his college sweetheart, another lawyer, and they started a family. It wasn't long before Jake's career, with its long hours and many community responsibilities, began taking its toll on his marriage. He was driven and determined, and he had begun to taste success. The more he tasted, the more he wanted.

That's about when his wife, Jessica, contacted me.

"We have every possible benefit a family could want except love," Jessica began. "Jake is a good provider. I work part-time, care for our children, and play golf with my friends. But I don't dare suggest Jake work less to be with us or ask about his investments. In fact, I don't dare say anything to Jake that he doesn't want to hear. Everyone in our community and church loves him. But I'm not sure where I fit in. I'm not married to a man; I'm married to a power machine."

"Money without love isn't worth much," I stated.

"You've got that right," she said sadly. "I don't think people really understand. They look at us and think we have it all."

"Have you spoken to others about this?" I asked.

"I don't have anyone to talk to," she said. "Everyone believes Jake is the best thing that ever happened to this community. He looks good, acts good...he's who they look up to. He's on the deacon board at church. In fact, he and the pastor are buddies. The pastor can't see any of these problems because he is just as powerful as Jake. He's the CEO of a 2000-member church and needs Jake."

"I can imagine," I said.

"So, you see how Jake and the pastor could feed each other's desire for success? He's an asset to his law firm, our city, our church, and I guess to us. But I have to sit silently watching things happen around me. He doesn't listen to my thoughts, so I quit trying to communicate. I hold everything in."

"How would you describe your marriage?" I asked.

"It's great if I don't tell him how awful I feel. If I do, he launches into an attack of how ungrateful I am for everything we have—and we have a lot. I feel guilty complaining to you about it now. I'm afraid to expose any of my feelings to anyone."

Jessica has some incredible challenges facing her. She lives in a million-dollar home, drives a fancy car, and hasn't a financial care in the world. In exchange, she keeps silent about not having an intimate connection with her husband.

Narcissists' Personality Plus

Although Jessica complained to me about her life, she had been pulled into Jake's powerful web one step at a time. Initially she felt drawn to his kindness and strength, but now she feels pushed away by his enormous life. She wanted to be cared for because of who she was, but now his attention to her comes in very small doses.

"Jake can be a wonderful man," she said, shifting in mood. "I really do love him, but I wonder if he is good for me. I knew he was going to make something of his life, and he has. I knew I could count on him to provide stability, and he has. But I didn't know the fun was going to evaporate. I didn't know the rules of the game were going to be dictated by him."

"What was it you fell in love with?" I asked. "What keeps you so attached to him?"

"Oh, that's easy," she said. "He was charismatic and a leader who could get anyone to follow him, and they did. I did."

She paused to answer the second part of the question.

"What keeps me attached?" she asked reflectively. "He is still a leader. He is strong where I feel weak. He is courageous where I feel fear. He is bold where I'm timid. I married him and believe in commitment. It's all so confusing."

As I listened to Jessica I couldn't help but wonder if she was really timid or if she had pushed down her feelings of strength for so long, she began to believe she was weak. Many women lose important aspects of their personality in the face of forcefulness.

In working with Jessica I am reminded of many of the narcissistic people I've worked with professionally. They rise to the top, gathering emotional and charismatic steam on their ascent. The higher they climb, the more attention they command. The more attention they command, the more powerful they feel.

"Jake can command any room," Jessica continued. "He gets

whatever he wants because he can convince anyone of anything. Who can compete with that?"

Power often contaminates our thinking. Powerful people start actually believing they are better than they are, bigger than they are, and more important than they are. Power combined with love is particularly intoxicating. Power without the constraints of accountability and morality—often found in narcissists—is dangerous, and this forces the mate to disappear!

Raw Power

Let's just put it out there: Jake is a narcissist and an emotionally abusive man. Let's look at what Jessica said about her husband.

"Jake can command any room."

What a statement! Can you sense Jessica's attraction and her fear? Can you feel her trepidation about making a mistake, her fear of his criticism—key aspects of emotional abuse? Can you imagine why she might have been attracted to Jake in the first place and why now, with a family, beautiful home, active church life, and strong place in her community, she would stay?

Mike Bundrant, in his article "10 Traits of Powerful People," offers a closer look at power and powerful people. Powerful people, he says, see power in you and expect you to live up to that power. They may believe in you more than you believe in yourself. Powerful people also see weaknesses in you and opportunities to exploit those weaknesses. They see a chance to be exactly who they want to be without resistance from you.

Bundrant goes on to say that powerful people cannot be easily manipulated. They know what they want. They often have clear goals, purpose, and direction and will set a path and stick to it.[1] Again, it is easy to see why we might be attracted to such a person.

The abuse of power has been prevalent throughout history. The Old Testament is replete with warnings about this.

- "You shall not rule over him with severity, but are to revere your God" (Leviticus 25:43 NASB).

- "You shall not oppress a hired servant who is poor and needy, whether he is one of your countrymen or one of your aliens who is in your land in your towns" (Deuteronomy 24:14 NASB).
- "Calling them to himself, Jesus said to them, 'You know that those who are recognized as rulers of the Gentiles lord it over them; and their great men exercise authority over them. But it is not this way among you, but whoever wishes to become great among you shall be your servant; and whoever wishes to be first among you shall be slave of all'" (Mark 10:42-44 NASB).

Oppression and abuse of power have always been severely warned against and are antithetical to the gospel. Power, privilege, and personality can be incredibly dangerous.

Power Envy

Jake abused power, and Jessica was hurt in the process. She probably wasn't the only one.

Jessica shared something fascinating with me.

"I admired Jake's confidence, and I wanted to share in it," she said. "I saw him move about with such ease, and I felt stronger being with him. I saw other people attracted to him, and I knew I would never have all that, but I could maybe have some of it by being with him."

She paused and then added, "At least at first. Now I'm just tired. I'm anxious all the time and feel crazy. When he tells me I should be thankful for everything we have, my head starts to spin."

I often tell clients they are likely in a crazy-making situation if they start to feel crazy. We are likely experiencing emotional abuse if we feel off center, confused, and slightly disoriented at times.

As I listened, I noticed Jessica's push-pull relationship with Jake and his power. She admires him and the impact he has on others (pull), but she feels smaller in relationship to him (push). Her weariness and anxiety have increased with each passing year. Perhaps you can relate. She appreciates his determination and abilities to go where he wants to go (pull) but hates that she's being bulldozed in the process (push). She admires his charm (pull) but hates his manipulation of her (push). Every positive, enviable trait seems to have such a harsh shadow side.

In the article "Envy: The Emotion Kept Secret," Dr. Mary Lamia shares that envy is a natural emotion, but it is often felt as ugly. Envy is triggered when we sense we are coming up short compared to others. In order to work through our envy, we often struggle to either diminish others, elevate ourselves, or both. We must perform a lot of mental gymnastics to silence the envy beast within.[2]

Jessica's admission—admiring and wishing for just a bit of her husband's confidence—is one I've heard many times. Many women are both attracted to and repulsed by the power of men. They want some of that power while they simultaneously push away from it. They like what power, prestige, and personality can get them, but ultimately they loathe the drawbacks that also come with the territory. Like a moth drawn to a flame, this struggle can be their undoing.

Perhaps you have these same feelings—wanting the benefits that come with his power while pushing away from the fears that come with his domination. You feel the perplexing ambivalence of wanting to run while being committed to stay.

Ultimately we would all do well to come to terms with our secret wish for power but also what comes with that power. Many of us have something in common with not only power-wielding men but also power-envying women. We would do well to step back and evaluate what is really important to us.

As with many other women, the balance sheet for Jessica lands in the minus column, with liabilities far outweighing assets. If she can gain the courage to set boundaries on the traits that are harmful to her, regaining her voice, she may be able to appreciate more of Jake's attributes as well as cultivating those same traits in herself.

Personality Plus Dangers

Can you see the dangers of a strong, winning personality? Can you feel yourself, your own integrity, slipping away, getting smaller and smaller in the shadow of his huge ego?

I've always considered emotional intelligence a critical aspect of the personality, a greater gift than brain power, but there has always been a dark side to an enchanting personality. Charisma—charm and influence with others—has its dangers, especially if that charisma is not harnessed or fully recognized. Consider someone you've known who was charming and manipulative.

Tomas Chamorro-Premuzic, in his article "The Dark Side of Charisma," cites four significant dangers of charisma.

1. *Charisma dilutes judgment.* He states there are only three ways to influence others: force, reason, and charm. He goes on to say that force and reason are rational, while charisma (charm) is based on emotional manipulation.
2. *Charisma is addictive.* He states leaders capable of charming their followers become addicted to their love. They crave approval, which detracts them from their actual goals. Followers, on the other hand, become addicted to the leader's charisma, leading to a reciprocal dependence.
3. *Charisma disguises psychopaths.* You don't have to be a psychopath to be charming, Premuzic says, but many psychopaths are charming. Egocentricity, deceit, manipulativeness, and selfishness are key aspects of many advancing leaders.
4. *Charisma fosters collective narcissism.* People are charmed by others only when they share values and principles. We don't find someone charismatic who is very different from ourselves.[3]

It is not hard to see these traits of charisma in the narcissist. This list is a warning of what happens when charisma and personality run amok. These dangers highlight how insidious narcissism and emotional abuse can be. Emotional abuse can be present with anyone who has a degree of charm, and we must be alert to these dangers. We must use sound judgment to determine whether someone is using his charm and personality for good (as President Roosevelt did) or harm (as Hitler did).

Money

Perhaps you've wondered if I would get around to the topic of money and how it relates to power, privilege, and personality. Many people like Jake have power, privilege, personality, and money. There is, without a doubt, some correlation between all these factors.

While having money is not a prerequisite to being a narcissist, people with money must guard against narcissism. You don't have to be emotionally abusive to have money, but wealthy people face more temptations to use their power against others.

Scripture offers this warning: "The love of money is a root of all kinds of evil. Some people, eager for money, have wandered from the faith and pierced themselves with many griefs" (1 Timothy 6:10).

The Scripture here is clear that *the love of money* is the issue, not money itself. An obsession with acquiring wealth is a self-feeding fire that consumes a person.

In my work with narcissists and emotionally abusive people, money is often in the mix. Again, money itself is not evil, and wealthy people can be emotionally healthy. Money doesn't have to corrupt. But in many instances, money feeds the narcissistic ego. Money is power, and power often hurts others.

The Incredible Draw

Power, money, privilege, and personality create an incredible draw. Many women have been seduced by this combination, losing their bearings and sometimes their sanity.

I repeat, there is an incredible draw to power, privilege, and personality. In his article "The Dangerous Attraction of Powerful Men," Mark Banschick emphasizes that the Kennedys, Bill Clinton, or Tiger Woods would not have been so successfully seductive had there not been an audience waiting to "be in love with love." "Would any of these men," he suggests, "have been so exploitative if they couldn't get away with it?"[4]

Look at King David, perhaps the greatest of biblical kings. David was ruthless in his quest for power, willing to send a man to his death so he could secure the man's wife, Bathsheba. We all know about his repentance and consequences of his sin, but in keeping with the culture of his day, little is mentioned about his abuse of power. He is a study in power, prestige, and personality with all their attractions and atrocities. When he functioned as a narcissist, he caused harm to everyone in his world.

King David, for all his faults, is a relatable figure. He is known as a man after God's heart. He rose in power and stature, fell under their lure and temptations, but ultimately had a broken and repentant heart. We see why women would be drawn to him and men would fear him. We also see how power was dangerously intoxicating and addictive. As a result, we watched him fall.

The Path Forward

This chapter has been sobering and perhaps a little discouraging. I'm laying out the dangers of narcissism. You must know first about the dangerous combination of power, privilege, and personality. After understanding this, you can begin to find a way to confront these issues.

While power, prestige, and personality are intoxicating, emotional sobriety is better. For as much bad press is out there, shouting that the emotionally abusive man cannot change and the narcissist is never willing to change, I offer hope. Amid the firestorm on the Internet and social media berating these men, I offer another path.

The path forward is one of further understanding, further challenge, and increased possibility. Power, privilege, and personality have their advantages but also great pitfalls. As we move forward, we will learn how humility and openness to change can open the doors to healing.

Join me as we now learn about falling in love with love, the vulnerabilities that make you susceptible to abuse, and how to guard yourself from abuse in the future.

3

Falling for Him Again

And now these three remain: faith, hope and love. But the greatest of these is love.

1 CORINTHIANS 13:13

I can remember exactly where I was when it happened. I know the year, the date, and definitely the setting. Mostly I remember the feeling. I wrote about it in the journal I was keeping at the time.

"January 20, 2003. I've met a wonderful woman," I wrote. "Her name is Christie, and she is cute, lively, engaging, and romantic. I want to see her again. We'll see what happens."

The setting was the small town of Port Orchard, Washington. I took Christie out to a movie—*Catch Me If You Can*. Our first date.

After a lovely evening complete with a movie, hors d'oeuvres, and friendly repartee, I was smitten. I felt my brain change as I admired this woman.

I remember looking at her and saying something like, "I'd like to date you again, if you're interested."

"Are you dating anyone else?" she asked.

"Yes," I said.

"That won't work for me," she said confidently. "You'll need to decide."

Decision made!

I had been in love before. I knew this feeling, and it was wonderful.

I knew I was about to enter a different world—a wonderful world where sights are more profound, sounds more intense, smells more delightful, and colors—oh, the magnificent colors!—are so beautiful.

I braced for impact and simultaneously let myself go. Like a ride at the carnival, sometimes you simply give in to the experience.

Since you're reading this book, you know this feeling too. You know the heady experience of falling in love. However, your story may not be going well.

Falling in Love with a Narcissist

I've shared my story so that you will know that I know about falling in love. I also tell you my story because I want you to think about love—specifically, you falling in love. What has happened in your life? How have you fallen in love? Has it been wonderful, or has it been filled with bumps and bruises?

This chapter is about our innate, God-given tendencies to fall in love. It is about the dangers that occur when those innate tendencies meet up with the dangers of the narcissistic, emotionally abusive man. You will learn about yourself, perhaps recognize yourself in some of the stories, and learn what you must do in the future. I will help you make sense of it all.

Janene contacted me after falling in love. In midlife, after a painful divorce and a short season of working on herself, she fell head over heels in love with her Realtor, Brian. Janene shared how she fell for Brian and married him six weeks later.

"I'm ashamed to tell you that I only knew him six weeks before we got married. It felt so right. I was a Christian and so was he. I was looking for a new house, and he was a recently divorced Realtor. He was kind, caring, compassionate, and a great dancer. After only two weeks he said either we get married or he was moving on. I couldn't believe it. He was dead serious and I thought, 'Oh well. Why not?'"

Just six months later Janene moved out. Her head was no longer dancing in ecstasy but swimming in agony.

"I left him because my life was like a bad roller-coaster ride—huge highs and frightening lows. He's like Dr. Jekyll and Mr. Hyde. He's the nicest guy you would ever want to meet—or the nastiest guy. I never knew which one was coming in the door."

Janene told me she felt instantly relieved after she left Brian. However, now four months later, Brian showed up with flowers, remorseful and "absolutely certain" they should be together, promising things will change.

"I miss him," she shared, "but I'm tired of everything. Am I making a mistake? I'm so confused. Can it work?"

"What are your reservations?" I asked.

"Well," she said slowly. "All the problems that were there before are still there. I'm afraid of my 'magical thinking,' as you call it, believing things will be different. He is still jealous of all my friends but hasn't ended his female friendships. He can be charming and demanding all at once. And he is still controlling and has a scary temper. My head is spinning."

Janene paused and began crying.

"I feel so pathetic," she said. "Look at me. I feel like a 13-year-old, and I'm 43. What is the matter with me? Why can't I just walk away from him? He's not good for me. I'm a Christian, and I think God wants me to be with him, but does God want me to be crazy? I am so confused."

Let's slow down and reflect on this all-too-common story. Feeling confused and utterly fatigued is common with women connected to emotionally abusive men. Feeling both exhausted and weary, women often settle for the status quo as change seems impossibly difficult. It's often easier to stay with something we know rather than make a change. It's hard work to step back and reflect on our lives, separating the good from the bad. Add feeling alone and the prospect of change seems even harder. Maybe even impossible.

Choosing Wisely

Janene was emotionally frozen, feeling tired and confused, making her situation even more difficult and leaving her vulnerable to making poor choices. It is hard to make wise choices when feeling bedraggled and worn.

Lundy Bancroft, in his book *Why Does He Do That?*, notes that women will often get hooked back into a relationship when they see a shred of hope.[1] So hungry for a positive sign, they naively believe things will be fine when that is not the case.

Janene had that naive hope. She needed to think long and hard about her situation. Her situation was layered with emotion, doubts, and fears. What she needed was professional counsel and the wise support of friends.

Unfortunately, when it comes to love, the consoling and counseling from friends and family is often simplistic and unreasonable. Some friends don't want to get involved. All are opinionated, which often stops them from listening well and simply offering support. Most don't really understand the addictive nature of toxic, troubled love.

Seeking wise counsel is critical. Scripture tells us, "Where there is no guidance the people fall, but in abundance of counselors there is victory" (Proverbs 11:14 NASB). Knowing who to listen to will not be an easy task. Janene needed clear instruction from a professional who knows about narcissism and emotional abuse. Even then, she must discern whether that counsel reflects her feelings and a thorough understanding of narcissism and emotional abuse.

Janene faced a mountain of questions. Why did she fall for a man who made her head spin? Why was she willing to get back on the roller coaster? We methodically looked at her history for explanations. We sought answers to questions about her vulnerability to a narcissistic man. Here's what her history showed.

Three years ago, Janene went through a painful, embittered divorce. The protracted proceedings left her wounded and afraid, scarred and scared. She now shares custody of her children with her ex, but she fears he may take her back to court anytime she does something he doesn't like. She is tiptoeing through life.

"It was ugly," she said, referencing her first marriage. "My husband drank a lot. Even though he lost his job and had a history of lying to me, the church wanted me to hang in there and pray for him to sober up. He never did, and I just couldn't take it. The divorce was messy, and I lost a lot of friends and even my church. It was terrible. I feel so guilty. I wonder if that is why I don't want to give up."

"I hadn't dated for a couple of years," Janene continued thoughtfully. "I knew I needed time to heal. Then I met Brian, and I was attracted to him immediately. And when he showed interest in me, it was an incredible feeling."

Now Janene felt ashamed, a common feeling of those falling for someone who turns out to be emotionally abusive. As we talked, Janene shared how she was taken in by his charm and delighted by both his success and admiration of her. It was easy to see how she could lose her emotional footing. Once you fall, it's very easy to move faster than you intended. The experience is a lot like high school love and every bit as emotionally intoxicating. She missed being cared about. She missed love.

Now What?

Janene jumped into a relationship without fully exploring the danger signs. She was vulnerable and settled before thoroughly examining her situation. She allowed her heart to be overwhelmed by his affection and attention.

But is it really that simple? Let's step back and explore what might have been happening inside her.

Janene had been seriously wounded from her divorce and years of trying to get her husband to choose her instead of alcohol. She left her marriage feeling fragile, broken, and terribly vulnerable, and she still wonders if she tried hard enough to save their marriage.

Many of us have had that profound feeling of being rejected. It is a terrible blow to the brain. Nearly all of us have been dumped by someone we love, and just as many of us have dumped someone who loved us. Yet we fight for love, yearn for love, pine for love. We write songs and poems and stories about love. We create mesmerizing films about love. For as complex as love is, for as many wounds as are created by it, we still yearn to be loved. We cling to love even when it involves a narcissist or emotionally abusive man. Love is complex and is wired into our DNA.

Perhaps the greatest treatise given on love is the love chapter in the Bible, which reads in part, "Love never fails. But where there are prophesies, they will cease; where there are tongues, they will be stilled; where there is knowledge, it will pass away...And now these three remain: faith, hope and love. But the greatest of these is love" (1 Corinthians 13:8,13).

Indeed, we were made for love, and it is the greatest. We have been relational since the beginning of time, and so it should not surprise us that Janene went against her best judgment and fell for Brian after such a short time. Love is intoxicating, life-giving, and so enjoyable. If we could bottle and sell it, we would be infinitely wealthy.

The Brain in Love

What does Janene's story teach us about love in general and emotional abuse in particular? So far you've learned that "the brain on love" is not necessarily healthy or rational. Romantic love is one of the most powerful sensations on earth. That obsession gets worse for those who have been rejected—that's 95 percent of us.

But what exactly happens to your brain when you meet this man who seems too good to be true? Why are you smitten and nearly unable to think straight? Do you remember the ad where a guy fries an egg and then states, "This is your brain on drugs"? As it turns out, researchers have now concluded "the effects of love on the brain are strikingly similar to the effects of drugs on it."[2]

Robert Weiss, in his article "This Is Your Brain on Love," writes that magnetic resonance imaging technology has discovered that...

- "Intense romantic love activates the striatum...a region of the brain that is often referred to as the pleasure center."
- "Romantic love also activates the insula, a region of the brain that assigns value to pleasurable and life-sustaining activities."[3]

Limerence—the short-term glue that keeps couples together long enough for long-term love to take place—depends on the blood flow to these areas of the brain.

Weiss cites other research that indicates the parts of the brain impacted by love are also the parts most heavily affected by addictive drugs. Yes, it turns out that limerence and love have much in common with cocaine and heroin. Lasting love and addictive substances have similar neurochemical underpinnings.

This may help you understand why people in love—you, perhaps—often appear obsessed and addicted, especially in the early stages of a new romance.[4] You were experiencing a neurochemical rush (a high) that made you want to stay in a relationship that may not have been good for you. It explains why some, such as Janene, fell fast and hard for someone who was ultimately not healthy for her.

More on Falling in Love

In my work with thousands of couples struggling with emotional abuse, the issue of falling in love has almost always been central. I've witnessed many people who, despite their best intentions, make poor choices again and again.

In one of the most profound books I've ever read, *The Road Less Traveled*, Scott Peck has much to say about falling in love.

> Of all the misconceptions about love the most powerful and pervasive is the belief that "falling in love" is love or at least is one of the manifestations of love. It is a potent misconception, because falling in love is subjectively experienced in a very powerful fashion as an experience of love.[5]

Peck notes that falling in love is almost always an act of regression. We are quite literally out of our minds. We feel a temporary sense of omnipotence. All problems can be overcome during this heady experience. But this intoxication fades, and the couple must get on with the work of real loving.

It is here that you wake up and begin to notice the danger signs. It is here that you feel that anxious pit in your stomach that maybe you have made a mistake. Your body records the emotionally abusive actions that are sometimes noticeable, sometimes not.

Peck helps us make more sense out of this experience. He notes that falling in love is not an act of the will or conscious choice. He notes that we may fall in love with someone not suited for us.

> We are as likely to fall in love with someone with whom we are obviously ill-matched as with someone more suitable…We can choose how to respond to the experience of falling in love, but we cannot choose the experience itself.[6]

In those thousands of couples I've worked with, nearly every person fell fast and hard for their mate. They loved being in love and wanted to perpetuate that feeling at all costs. Like the addict seeking drugs, many of the individuals sought to maintain the relationship even though in retrospect they remember seeing warning signs.

Love Bombing

You've learned about you in love and how vulnerabilities set us up to make poor choices. Let's shift now to the narcissist. What is he up to? What is his part in you falling in love again? There's a good chance you've been the victim of *love bombing*.

Reflect back to the early days of love. Something probably happened that should have set off a red flare. Janene was swept off her feet by love bombing—being showered with praise and gifts and adoration. Remember that she was vulnerable, having been hurt deeply in her marriage and subsequent divorce.

She meets Brian, who knows how to treat a woman. He tells her she is the best thing that has ever happened to him, and she is totally unlike anything he's ever experienced before. He studies her and reflects what she wants to see and hear. He watches her closely, always noting what she is looking for, which feels very flattering. He is a perfect chameleon, able to mimic her emotions and blend into her desires.

When love bombing, the narcissist appears teachable, humble, hungry to know you, and fascinated by you. He may be very spiritual and able to use that language. He continually speaks of how special you are and how different you are from anyone else he's known. He's lavish and poetic and flattering. His whole world is about studying you. Later, however, he will use all he's learned to control you.

Now, to be fair, I'm not suggesting that every man is a narcissist or that every narcissist wakes up in the morning and sets out to conquer a woman. Many believe all narcissists are diabolical and vile, seeking to manipulate and overwhelm women. Yet I have found many are actually genuine, although often shallow in both intentions and attentions. They may truly care for you and feel swept off their feet. They may have no conscious ulterior motives, and only time reveals their true character.

To be found irresistible is irresistible, and the narcissist knows this! It is nearly impossible to resist love bombing, as Brittany Wong warns us in her article "9 Signs You're in Love with a Narcissist."

> Narcissists are very, very good at turning on the charm when they first meet you. As far as they're concerned, you've got the looks of a young Elizabeth Taylor and the wit of a thousand Tina Feys. But don't get used to those compliments or the pricey dinners they treat you to—it's not likely to last...That behavior is called love bombing, but with a narcissist, the smothering, razzle-dazzle display has nothing to do with you. You merely supply whatever the narcissist wants at the time (sex, money, status, youth). Once he or she has you, the "love" you feel will morph into control and denigration.[7]

Think about it. Who can resist being adored, told they are wonderful, incredible? Who can push away from receiving lavish gifts? We are all susceptible to admiration, and many narcissists have a keen sense of who is more vulnerable than another and likely to be susceptible to these gestures.

Vulnerability and Love

In a perfect world, we would be secure, clear about our identity, and able to recognize the narcissist's lavish attention for the shallowness that it is. We would feel emotionally strong, spiritually protected, and balanced in our judgment. We would not be so vulnerable to the narcissist.

But we don't live in a perfect world. We live in a world of insecurity and sometimes abject fear. We have a history of wounds, triggered again by rejection. Even though we guard these vulnerable aspects of our personality, we can do only so much to remain safe.

We are a mosaic of parts: part secure and clear, part confused and uncertain, part downright frightened. We all have a history, and for many victims of narcissistic and emotional abuse, that history includes being significantly wounded. This creates vulnerability that you must come to understand and do your utmost to heal.

Vanessa, another client, is a perfect reflection of this mosaic. She called me one evening in a panic after she and her boyfriend split up. She and I had been working together for a couple of years.

Vanessa owns an accounting business and conducts herself with strength and courage in her professional life. But in her personal life she feels embarrassed and ashamed that she has allowed herself to be mistreated. She has not even confided in her closest friends about her problems.

"Brad got mad over something trivial and broke up with me again," she said. "I'm so sick of this," she cried. "I'm better than all of this drama, but for some reason I keep allowing him to leave when he gets mad and then return when he's over it. When he's over it he wants to pretend nothing happened, and I just go along with it.

"The cycle is always the same," she continued. "He breaks up with me and stays away for days. He's even hooked up with other women. Then when he's done being upset, he comes back to me very loving and showers me with attention. So I forget about feeling hurt and fall for him all over again. It doesn't seem to take long before he's back to being his angry self again. By then I'm hooked and don't have the courage to talk about the fight or his behavior. It's all crazy."

Over the next few sessions we began exploring Vanessa's history, paying special attention to her personality traits of both strength and vulnerability. We discussed the cycles of behavior she was beginning to recognize and how to use that information to her advantage.

Love and Emotional Abuse

Vulnerability is a key issue when learning about love and emotional abuse. Narcissists cannot be narcissistic if they don't have someone to manipulate. They are adept at finding a vulnerable woman in the crowd. This is in no way said to cast any blame or shame on you. Rather, this book has been written to empower and strengthen you.

I am often asked by victims of emotional abuse, "If he really loved me, how could he do what he is doing to me?" A variation of this question is, "Does he really love me?"

These are powerful questions asked by women who have suffered from narcissistic victim's syndrome and emotional abuse. I do not use the word "suffer" lightly, as I've seen women who have been suicidal or whose physical health has been compromised from being mistreated psychologically by their mate.

What is going on here? How can love and abuse be part of the same relationship?

Think about the love of a six-year-old. A narcissist's love is immature, able to love but not love well. A six-year-old certainly has the capacity to care for others, but their caring is phenomenally self-absorbed. They care about what you can do for them, not what they can do for you. They become easily frustrated when not getting what they believe they deserve. They demand their way, lose their temper, and act out. They have little capacity to sit and listen to you. Rather, they want to be listened to, perhaps even demanding attention.

Love and emotional abuse sadly can and often do go together, ultimately because emotionally abusive behaviors are often part of the character structure of many men. With their vulnerable egos threatened, these men relate as emotional boys. Unable to deal effectively with their emotional pain and feeling easily threatened, their emotional abuse is often a symptom of a deeper problem—unhealthy strategies used for self-protection.

When their ego is threatened in some way, narcissists are likely to employ one or more of these emotionally abusive tactics.

- *Powering over.* This has also been called "power play," when one forces their will on another. "This is going to go my way, and that's all there is to it."

- *Scapegoating.* Putting the burden of responsibility onto an innocent person and placing themselves in the favorable light. "I didn't do anything wrong. It was all their fault."
- *Minimizing.* Treating another as a lesser individual or treating actions as less severe than they are. "What I did wasn't that big of a deal."
- *Playing the victim.* Making it seem as if the perpetrator is the one being wronged instead of the real victim. "Nothing I do is ever good enough."
- *Blame shifting.* Taking the onus off the perpetrator of harm and putting it onto the victim. "It's your fault, not mine. I haven't done anything you haven't done."
- *Excuse making.* Making supposedly rational explanations for inexcusable actions, failing to take responsibility for misbehavior. "I didn't mean to do it. It was an accident."
- *Rage reactions.* Erupting in overt or covert anger—this could take the form of passive-aggressive actions or outright rage. "This is intolerable and inexcusable, and I won't stand for it."
- *Stonewalling.* Retreating into silence. "I'm not talking to you."
- *Shunning.* Intentionally discontinuing contact with a person because of dislike for their justifiable actions. "Don't ever talk to me again."
- *Justification.* Offering an allegedly reasonable excuse for inexcusable actions. "What I did is really understandable. Just listen to me!"
- *Rewriting history.* Disavowing knowledge for having done a harmful action. "That's not what happened. I remember it completely different."

- *Deception.* Lying about an action to place themselves in a more favorable light. "I didn't do it."
- *Gaslighting.* Excuses, deflections, and justifications used to take the focus off the harmful behavior. "I don't remember it that way. I think you've got things all mixed up, which is what you always do."
- *Magical thinking.* Believing everything will work out without any real effort. "Everything will be fine. We can work this out. It shouldn't be too hard. I'm sure change will just happen."

Unfortunately, this is just a partial list of self-protective maneuvers—defenses—used to guard the faltering ego against any perceived assault. It is a good starting place though, and one we will refer to again in this book.

Trauma Bonding

"Why didn't I see it? Why didn't I listen? How could I fall for such a man?" These are the resounding questions asked by many victims of emotional abuse.

The answers are far more complex than you might think. There is a dynamic taking place with victims of abuse that is very concerning and one that you must understand. The dynamic occurring in most abusive relationships is *trauma bonding.*

What exactly is trauma bonding? Trauma bonding is a destructive attachment to someone harmful to us. This superglue attachment occurs where there is a mixture of good and bad, harm and health. This mixture can make a victim draw even closer to the one harming her. This occurs in emotionally abusive relationships in which the victim, being so controlled by the abuser, also sees him as her rescuer.

Trauma bonding explains how a victim of abuse comes to the defense of her man. We see it at play in her willingness to protect him even when she begins to see the abuse. Compound that with post-traumatic stress disorder and other chronic stress issues, and the bond becomes nearly impenetrable. The combination of love and disgust, grace and guilt, clarity and confusion, creates a most powerful adhesive to the relationship and to the abuser.

Trauma bonding, combined with the abusive defense tactics used to preserve and protect the narcissist's ego, are lethal to the woman trying to maintain her emotional footing. A little bit of abuse goes a very long way to creating confusion in the victim, causing her to seriously question if love ever truly existed in the relationship.

Janene and Vanessa's heads are spinning. For as much as they are being victimized, they are also being told that they are causing their marital problems, that they are the reason their marriages are not doing well. Remember the power of shame and the desire to keep everything secret. The power of shame is completely debilitating.

Their world has been managed and controlled down to meaninglessness. Their world is now filled with confusion as they have increasingly been defined by someone else—the narcissist. They live in fear, and that fear is now a defense—a way of coping. They would feel as if they were risking everything to let someone see into this world. Subsequently, many victims live in isolation, afraid to ask for help.

Bring the church into the mix, and we might inadvertently further strengthen the trauma bond. Janene and Vanessa feel conflicted in different ways about honoring God. Having been told that submission is the key to living a godly life and that the institution of marriage is paramount to a love relationship, they receive confusing messages and wonder how to heal.

Lost in Love

It is time to stop being lost in love. It is time to critically review your history of falling in love and be honest with yourself about relationships. It is important to determine whether your relationships have been healthy and life-giving or you have given up too much of yourself in the process.

Finding your way is about differentiating love from infatuation and healthy love from insecure dependency. It is about finding your way out of being lost in love, which leaves you worse than when you started. It is about gaining knowledge, getting clear, and preparing for making healthier choices.

Finding your way is also about learning how you have been mesmerized, showered with attention and affection, only to feel the pain and rejection that often follows. You've begun to see the dark side of the narcissist and can be far more mindful going forward. Your wisdom and insights are going to help you build a wonderful life.

The Path Forward

The path forward is far more certain than the path you have been on. You now understand whether you are in a trauma bond with your mate. You no longer have to be lost in love. With this understanding you will be equipped to move forward with greater confidence.

So let's begin learning about the fragile psyche, the easily wounded boy, that gives rise to the abusive man. As you understand him and perhaps even learn to care for him in new ways, you will learn better how to care for yourself.

4

How Dare You Say That!

Often, those who bruise easily spend too much time thinking about themselves.

MARIELLA FROSTRUP

I heard the same complaint yet again.

"This relationship is making me sick," Sheila said emphatically. "One day he's Mr. Wonderful, and the next day I feel like I'm raising another little boy. I'm tired of it."

I looked over at her husband, Brent, wondering how he'd respond to her harsh statement.

"Why do you say that, Sheila?" I asked.

"He's touchy. He's irritable. He has to have everything his way or I'm in trouble. I can't live like this."

Brent sat silently.

"Every woman coming to the Marriage Recovery Center says something like that. They are tired of tiptoeing around their husbands. Tell me more."

"His moods are unpredictable," she added. "I never know what to expect. Will Brent be the kind man who seems to care about me? Or will he be wrapped up in his world, thinking only about what makes him happy?"

Brent still sat silently, appearing more annoyed.

"I presume you've heard this before, Brent," I said. "Would you like to comment?"

"I don't think anything can make her happy," he said gruffly. "I work hard and come home tired. If I'm not Mr. Happy, she gets upset. She's the one with the moods if you ask me."

"I do like your good moods, Brent," she said. "But the point is I don't know when your mood is going to turn. So I'm just as fearful of the good times because I know it's going to end soon. It always does."

Brent shrugged and turned away. "Nothing I say is going to help."

"You could say something, Brent," she said. "I'd like you to at least acknowledge that we're talking about you. We're talking about our marriage."

"I don't know what to say," he said. "You're not happy, but what about me? I'm not sure I can make you happy anymore."

"I've told you, Brent," she said angrily. "That's why we're separated."

We continued on with the first session, talking about what led to Sheila and Brent's separation. Sheila had finally had enough. She was tired of trying to anticipate his moods. She was tired of Brent's short temper, never knowing what would upset him. Most important, Sheila was tired of trying to fit into Brent's life. She was weary of changing her behavior to fit the mold he expected her to fit into. She was losing her life one small piece at a time.

"Do you understand what she is saying, Brent?" I asked. "Do you know why she says she is losing her life?"

"Why are you asking me that?" he snapped.

Caught off guard, I wasn't sure what to say next. I could sense his agitation. "Are you upset by the question?"

"I don't like the question at all," he said, glaring at me. "I don't really want to be here, and don't like the direction this is going. She's going to try to blame me for everything. Nothing I do is ever good enough."

I certainly didn't want to start things off on the wrong foot. I was a bit anxious as this occurred in the first day of a three-day marriage intensive.

Suddenly Brent stood up and walked toward me.

"You asked me to understand her, but why don't you ask her to understand me? This intensive is not going to be all about me being bad. She's got changes to make too. You don't need to make me look stupid."

I felt myself reel back in my chair as if hit by a physical blow.

Sheila looked at me. "This is my life," she said, exasperated. "I don't know if our marriage can be saved."

Easily Offended

Whatever happened to me at that moment happens to women like Sheila every day. They are in love with a man who can be wonderful, but they are afraid of the hurt little boy who can be mean—all in the same person. What I witnessed was sensitivity gone bad. This is what the textbook means when it says the narcissist is likely to be easily offended—and that is what this chapter is about.

There was nothing I could say to completely save the situation. When an abusive man is offended, rarely can you say something magical to settle him down.

What I had experienced is called *personalization*. According to Dr. John M. Gohol, "Personalization is a distortion where a person believes that everything others do or say is some kind of direct, personal reaction to the person. We also compare ourselves to others trying to determine who is smarter, better looking, etc."[1] Personalization is often considered by many professionals as the mother of all guilt.

I was surprised at how I felt. Brent was angry and accusatory, and my mind whirred to discover ways to settle him down. This feeling—inadequate to settle a fiery situation—is what many women like Sheila live with.

I decided Brent had been very provocative, inciting me to feel guilty. Blame has that impact on everyone. He affixed blame onto me with the sheer power of his quick temper. He had taken his own feelings of inadequacy and projected them onto me—and it hurt.

I wondered how Sheila coped with such a man. How could she withstand his angry tirades? More specifically, how could she maintain emotional balance when he was so accusatory and touchy?

Sensitive? Not So Much

Poor Brent. He had to be feeling very vulnerable to be so reactive, right? While it is tempting to think of men like Brent as being hypersensitive, this may not be accurate. In some ways, he is. In other ways, not so much. What do I mean?

The "nice Brent" could certainly be sensitive. I'm sure he was capable of being kind and sensitive when things were going his way. But when things didn't go his way, he was likely to behave like the six-year-old we discussed.

If we looked at men like Brent through a normal lens, then it would be normal to be wounded when someone like me questions him. It's normal to react to a perceived slight. Sensitive people feel hurt when slighted.

However, men like Brent aren't thinking rationally. Brent has learned to react to any perceived slight. They have learned they have power and have learned to use it to control others. They use their aggression to make sure you back off and stay off—very primitive ways to maintain emotional balance.

So yes, men like Brent are hypersensitive. They perceive slights that no one intends. They react to issues that aren't issues at all. They see intentions when intended actions are not there. They read people's minds, judge their thoughts, and are ready to react. Having perceived an intended slight, they come out angry and aggressive.

Men like Brent are sensitive in a way, but they also are aggressors on the hunt for anyone who dares question them. They must feel superior, in charge. They will hurt anyone who dares to hurt them—and this makes them dangerous.

Impossible Expectations

It is impossible to predict how men like Brent will react. Will you encounter the charming man or the immature boy? I couldn't have known Brent would come at me for asking certain questions. Even with my extensive experience, men like Brent take me off guard. With impossible expectations, I flounder and fumble at times, which is the reaction they get from nearly everyone.

It is as if they are shouting, "Don't ever insult me. Don't ever upset me. Don't ever make me feel stupid."

Men like Brent don't let us off easy. They don't allow us the grace of thinking we didn't do something very wrong to them. They have convinced themselves, and attempt to convince us, that they are sensitive and we have done something terribly wrong to them. We have hurt them. It's as if we should have known better. Shame on us!

This is the roller coaster many women describe. They can never predict how their emotionally abusive mate will act. They can never satisfy all the requirements proclaimed by the childish tyrant.

Try as you might, you'll never assuage all his anger, and tragically, you may lose yourself trying. Women become exhausted trying to keep up with their man's demands, losing themselves and their sanity in the process. This physical and emotional exhaustion, perhaps more than anything, are hallmarks of emotional abuse.

Backpedaling

Isn't it amazing how intimidated we all feel when these emotionally abusive men come at us? It's crazy. We're the ones who have been beaten up by them, yet they are forever screaming about having been mistreated.

According to Kathleen Krajco, blog writer of "Narcissists Hypersensitive? To What?," narcissists are actually predators.

> We know that animal predators aren't (counter) attacking their prey in retaliation for any offense, don't we? How do we know that? Because the predator doesn't stop attacking when the prey tries to flee...
>
> And it's the same with narcissists. They can't be attacking in retaliation for any offense. Because they too just intensify their attack when the other party backs down, tries to appease, tries to flee, or shows any other sign of weakness. Just like an animal predator does.[2]

Is Krajco overstating the situation? Possibly, but I do see a significant degree of aggression in the wounded narcissist and emotionally abusive man. Like Brent, they are always on high alert. Watchful and wary, they react and overreact. Their mate is in a constant state of trauma, being stunned and stymied, worried and weary. With such reactivity, women remain frustrated and confused.

Victim or Villain

So is Brent a victim or a villain? Is he a wounded little boy, sensitive and hurt, or a predator to be watched closely?

The answer to this question is not as simple as you might think. What if his many emotional triggers, which render him ready to feel wounded, are caused by his own history of having been victimized? What if he is both a victim *and* a villain?

Brent was put on alert by my questioning. He was emotionally triggered and ready to react. He carries a huge insecurity button ready to be pushed. He is always afraid others are better than him, and everyone and everything they say runs the risk of pushing that button. Always feeling insecure and frightened, he walks through the world more vulnerable than his appearance lets on. In this sense he is a victim of his own wounded past.

Brent is also a villain, ready and willing to hurt others if that's what makes him to feel superior and safe. Feeling entitled and self-righteous, he looks down on others. He walks with a false sense of superiority to compensate for his suppressed feelings of inferiority. Narcissistic and immature, he uses others' empathy to get away with aggression.

How does he do this?

He does this the same way other narcissistic, emotionally abusive men do it. Feeling wounded or slighted, they turn on the person who confronts them to make them feel small and to make themselves feel superior. Were they slighted? Yes. Was it of any consequence? Not likely. The narcissist plays on others' empathic need to *not* hurt people. He has learned, at some primitive level, he has the power to make others obey him. He has learned that others will feel bad for what they have said or done. In this respect, narcissists are certainly villains.

Can you see the power in their actions? Can you feel the sense of grandiosity narcissists wield to manipulate others to bend to their whims? They broadcast nonverbal and verbal cues about being easily offended so that others will walk carefully around them.

Certainly Brent was a powerful man, attested to by the fact that his wife and I were reacting so cautiously around him. He was not the victim he was protesting himself to be, but now we were the victims of his defensive tactics.

Wounded Little Boy

Brent was certainly not a victim. Narcissists and emotionally abusive men have learned some very maladaptive behavior. Grossly immature, they think and behave like little boys, with their behavior being reinforced time and again.

Dr. Sam Vaknin, in his book *Malignant Self Love*, suggests narcissists are men who refuse to grow up. They are self-centered, haughty, demanding brats. Well-adjusted individuals seek to face life's challenges and mature, but narcissists and emotionally abusive men avoid emotional challenges. They avoid honestly dealing with the relationship challenges we all face that enable us to grow up.

Vaknin asserts, "The narcissist is a partial adult. He seeks to avoid adulthood. Infantilization—the discrepancy between one's advanced chronological age and one's retarded behavior, cognition, and emotional development—is the narcissist's preferred art form."[3]

Why would anyone avoid growing up? At first this doesn't make sense. Don't we all want to become the best version of ourselves possible?

Although critical of Brent, I saw bits of myself in him and was shocked. I recognized his pouting and manipulation. I can relate to Brent and other men who are emotionally underdeveloped. There are days when I don't want to grow up. There are times when I'm a bundle of raw emotion and want to react to my wife. Thankfully, more often than not, I interrupt these immature tendencies. But I have them.

Why are men like Brent so easily wounded?

Aubyn De Lisle, in her article "The Wounded Self—The Torture of Narcissism," notes that many of us feel discomfort when we admit something we feel ashamed about. Sharing information about our secret selves is freeing, however. Not so with the narcissist.

> At the other end of the scale is the person who has a constant sense of their own weakness and resentment at being the victim in the face of mistreatment by others. This, too, is a wound to the self which constantly battles with the need for validation. The person with true narcissistic personality disorder will not be able to tolerate that discomfort at all, to the extent that they simply will not recognize it as an issue.[4]

Wounded very early in life by strict, abusive fathers, abandonment, or sometimes profound neglect, these men limp through life. They experienced trauma and failed to develop a healthy sense of self. Needing a safe environment in which to develop and learn critical relationship skills needed as adults, these children have been robbed. The result is a selfish, demanding man-boy.

You know this is true. The empathic part of your personality wants to reach out and save him. When he is small and vulnerable you want to take him under your wings and let him know everything will be all right. You sense his fragility and want to protect him. When he turns on the charm, he is all the more likeable.

Like most little boys, he seems to intuitively know when he can be mean and when he must behave. He knows if he pushes too far, you will run, and in the end he cannot live without you.

Walking in Her Shoes

Sometime later I sat alone with Sheila to discuss how she was coping. I wondered what it was like to be with this victim-villain on a day-in, day-out basis. What was it like to be with someone she loved, someone who said he loved her but seemed to purposely hurt her?

"I'm so tired of the fights after the fights," she said.

"What do you mean?" I asked.

"There is always a fight after the fight. He never owns up to the problems he has created, so I have to either argue with him or give up. More and more I just give up. It's exhausting."

I have worked with many women who have been emotionally

abused and share the same sentiments. Even those with strong faith backgrounds struggle, often feeling compelled to tolerate any kind of treatment. Most feel completely confused and emotionally drained.

Tearfully Sheila shared the turning point for her emotionally.

"I was able to put up with his little-boy ways for a while, but then I really thought about the impact it was having on me and our two children. It was the thought that our kids were likely to pick up many of his traits that changed things for me. That made me think seriously about setting limits. I'm to the point now where if he is unwilling to change I may divorce him. I'm preparing myself for that."

I shared that I understood her decision, though truthfully I cannot say I really did. How can anyone other than the ones walking this path say they fully understand?

I summarized what I had noticed in the sessions thus far. I was uneasy with her husband in my short time with him, wary of how he might react to my interventions. I need to feel safe in order to offer emotional help, and he made it clear that he could not or would not tolerate confrontation. With me, as with his wife, he demanded admiration and attention.

It was critical at this point for me to share with Sheila that the counseling process could become tense. I would not be offering them good therapy if I didn't point out obvious concerns. I could not tiptoe around issues, specifically his reactivity, and do good therapy. If I enabled his power, I would be revictimizing her.

Sheila encouraged me to do the work I needed to do, to confront the bad behavior that needed confrontation. It was imperative that we not succumb to his abuse of power and manipulation. She was ready for whatever might happen.

Warning Signs

Sheila said she was ready for change and encouraged me to be confrontational. I encouraged her to be strong as well. Change was necessary if she was to have a healthy marriage. Maintaining the status quo was a sure way to ensure nothing changed.

Sheila is struggling to set boundaries on narcissistic and emotional abuse. A major aspect of her healing is to critically review what has caused her head to spin. She must first learn to recognize the warning signals that her husband and others like him transmit. She must learn about normal, healthy behavior and contrast that with unhealthy, abnormal, emotionally abusive behavior. Gaining freedom means discerning the good from the bad, the loving gestures from power and control tactics.

Perhaps you too are trying to decipher how you could stay in relationship with an abusive man. You might think it would be relatively easy to distinguish between a healthy man and an unhealthy one. No, it's not that easy.

Fortunately, there are warning signs. There are ways you can become smarter so that you can differentiate between healthy and unhealthy interactions, between mature love and immature, self-centered love. Consider some of these warning signs as you discern healthy love from malignant love.

Craig Malkin outlined this list in his article "5 Early Warning Signs You're with a Narcissist":

1. *Projected feelings of insecurity.* The narcissist and emotional abuser has a need to make others feel small out of his own incredible feelings of insecurity. Narcissists, with such a fragile ego, perceive any affront as overwhelming to them and watch for anything they can turn around on their mate.

2. *Emotion phobia.* The narcissist and emotional abuser has a hard time allowing himself to be touched by the emotions of others. Many of the narcissistic men I work with struggle to understand and name their feelings.

3. *A fragmented family story.* The narcissist and emotional abuser is typically insecurely attached and is unable to weave a coherent story of his past. He may idolize his family of origin or give contradictory messages about it. Many narcissists in my practice come from very

dysfunctional backgrounds with histories of neglect and brokenness.

4. *Idol worship.* The narcissist and emotional abuser often idolizes someone until that person comes crashing to earth. Then, sorely disappointed, the narcissist rejects the person who caused his disillusioned feelings. Most narcissists vacillate between idolizing people in their world and denigrating them.
5. *A high need for control.* The narcissist and emotional abuser fails to allow others to have their own preferences. Narcissists are highly controlling, demanding that other people behave the way they want.[5]

These warning signs offer a starting place for trying to sort out what has happened up to this point and learning how to make better choices for your future. Understanding these warning signs will help you distinguish between healthy and unhealthy men. This list can also point you in the direction of issues that need to be addressed should you choose to stay with your mate.

So Much Insecurity

Emotional abuse in its many forms is driven by deep-seated insecurity. This insecurity is no excuse for bad behavior. However, considering what is happening below the surface can help you to know how to respond and ultimately become healthy again. These men can grow up, when forced to.

Michael J. Formica has written an insightful article titled "Understanding the Dynamics of Abusive Relationships." He says,

> Abusive relationships are fairly simple. They are driven by insecurity, fear that feeds that insecurity and an expectation of inconsistency, both real and perceived.
>
> An abuser is morbidly insecure. S/he has little sense of his/her own social value and makes an effort to gain or re-gain

> some semblance of that value through domination and control. The fear that feeds that insecurity has two fronts: fear of not being lovable, and fear of appearing weak. The paradox here is that the abuser is, in fact, weak, which is why s/he abuses—to maintain a sense of control—in the first place.[6]

Formica nailed it. It is about control for the narcissist and emotional abuser. It is also about his fear of not being lovable. His behavior reinforces his fear. As he behaves poorly, he ultimately meets with both social and relational rejection. He has a sense that many don't like him. He feels this rebuff and reacts with even greater efforts to control.

Formica doesn't stop with observations about the abuser. He notes that victims suffer from severe insecurity as well. Victims have little sense of their own social value and gain value by submitting to the abuser's demand for domination. Victims are willing to accept the scraps of love and attention in place of the real thing out of their own insecurity.[7]

Victims and abusers find each other. The abuser needs control and the victim needs love and attention. They become accustomed to this kind of relationship, so it can be quite enduring. Many abusive relationships can be described as simply as that.

Caring and the Church

You might wonder about the role of the church in the issue of emotional abuse. Unfortunately, the church often unwittingly reinforces many of these troubling dynamics. The church is a body of loving, caring people who are ready to reach out to the needy, and you can't find someone needier than the wounded boy-man. Yet rather than challenge these men to grow up and be leaders in their homes, the church may coddle the boy in him by staying silent under the guise of not scaring him away or making sure he doesn't feel rejected.

The church must change. We must change. What we are currently doing is not working.

Many victims of emotional abuse find their faith confusing. If the church fails to take a clear stand on emotional abuse, many victims are left wondering, where is the boundary between loving and giving on one hand, and losing their lives to abuse on the other?

A simplistic reading of Scripture can add to this confusion.

The apostle Peter implores us, "Above all, love each other deeply, because love covers over a multitude of sins. Offer hospitality to one another without grumbling" (1 Peter 4:8-9). An emotionally vulnerable reader might naively assume this means she should give, give, and give some more, without limits.

Similarly, Jesus Himself tells us, "Whoever finds their life will lose it, and whoever loses their life for my sake will find it" (Matthew 10:39). A bewildered victim might equate that with enduring a husband's sinful abuse, though of course Jesus is saying nothing of the sort. We aren't here to pay the price of another's sin. Christ already did that. We are here to be salt and light. If we allow abuse as an acceptable way of life, we are actually participating in a cover-up rather than shedding light in a dark place.

Still, in their confusion and pain, women like Sheila can easily misinterpret passages like these. Thankfully, Scripture does *not* tell us to sit with abuse. Scripture does not sanction any kind of abuse. In 1 Corinthians 13 we read that love "does not dishonor others, it is not self-seeking, it is not easily angered, it keeps no record of wrongs...It always protects" (1 Corinthians 13:4-7). Certainly, our mate might like to remind us that love keeps no record of wrongs! And yet the most unloving thing we could do is enable them to thrive in their sin.

Scripture is clear that we are the crown of God's creation. "You have made them a little lower than the angels and crowned them with glory and honor" (Psalm 8:5). We were created to reflect God's richness and to join Him in the ongoing work of creation.

With Scripture offering us wisdom about how to proceed on the issue of emotional abuse, we need the church to lead the way. The church must not tolerate any form of abusive behavior. These are boundaries that must be reinforced as designed by God.

Who's Responsible for His Bad Feelings?

Getting clear about who is responsible for whom is perhaps the most critical decision you can make. God designed us to be caring—*not* to coddle emotionally wounded, abusive men.

As I reflected on my reaction with Brent, I realized that I had rescued him. I had decided that he needed to be handled softly. I had put my own desire not to rile him ahead of what was appropriate—which was to confront his behavior. I had decided that I needed to walk softly to keep him in counseling. Wrong! Failing to call out bad behavior, victimizing Sheila again, would not save her or their marriage. Confronting unhealthy behavior would give them a chance at a healthy marriage.

After my initial mistake, I changed my mind. I decided that Brent must not be enabled to treat me or his mate badly. He must learn that bad behavior is bad. Though he may be hurting, it's not okay to hurt others. Though wounded and insecure, he cannot bully his way in the world.

Living this out with Brent won't be easy. I don't have any quick answers, but I'm prepared to confront him with his troubling actions. I've encouraged Sheila to stand firm in not tolerating abuse. She is prepared to live this out as well, making it clear that any reconciliation would be based on him growing up and treating her well. We both realized we are not responsible for his behavior. He alone is responsible for how he treats others, and this will play a huge role in how others treat him.

The Path Forward

Shelia is beginning to live a different life with Brent. His narcissism and emotional abuse will not save their marriage. Sheila is stronger and is acting on her God-given wisdom and clarity.

Brent does not like her new behavior and firmer boundaries. He maintains a grudge and has not yet made a significant change in his heart that would lead to change in his behavior. Yet with firmer boundaries in place, change is now possible. The choice is his.

Once you have clearer boundaries in place, you too will be prepared to move forward. You know more about your mate's insecurities, which drive his troubling behavior. You have learned about warning signs for abusive behavior. You have also learned that God is not asking you to suffer in an abusive relationship. He has a much better life designed for you.

Let's move ahead now into understanding narcissistic victim syndrome. Together we will explore the impact of chronic abuse and ways to recover from it.

5

Narcissistic Victim Syndrome

You can either be a victim of the world or an adventurer in search of treasure. It all depends on your view of life.

PAULO COELHO

Victim.

The word conjures up many images for most people.

When I hear the word "victim," I immediately visualize someone robbed at gunpoint, beaten by a group of thugs, or swindled out of their lifetime savings by an unethical stock broker.

I don't visualize a 35-year-old woman who is married to a soft-spoken small-business owner and who complains about how he treats her. I don't think of a 50-year-old woman whose husband is the high school coach and respected throughout the community for his generosity but who runs his home like an NFL football team.

Victim.

Most of us don't quite know what to do with this word, the concept, or the actual person. We don't have a place in our minds and emotional life for a woman continually beaten by attitudes, words, and actions. We are not sure what to say to her, whether to advise her to stay or leave him.

As a result of this phenomenal lack of comprehension, many women, abjectly alone, are floundering on their own to find support. They typically suffer in silence, unable to define what is happening to them. After years living silently with this threat, they may begin seeking help to understand their experience.

This happens, however, only after suffering alone and beginning a downward spiral of poor emotional and physical health.

Victim.

This chapter will help you become a bit more comfortable not only with the word but with the possibility that you are struggling with a cluster of symptoms known as narcissistic victim syndrome (NVS). We will examine what is happening to you and many other women.

A Woman's Story

Debra is one of many women struggling with narcissistic victim syndrome (NVS), a nonclinical diagnosis for women who have been victimized by a narcissist. There are as many different stories as there are women victimized by their emotionally abusive men.

Debra was an elementary school teacher for years, though her career was cut short by the myriad physical symptoms of her diagnosis. She struggled with fatigue, anxiety, and confusion and simply could not continue with the work she loved.

"I never know what the day is going to bring," she said. "I have to take it one day at a time. I'm afraid to plan anything for the future, so it was impossible to keep my job."

"What is your typical day like?" I asked.

"There is no typical day, but I will probably be downright weary. I know I will probably ache all over. My brain will probably be in such a fog that I can't make the simplest of decisions. It's all so discouraging."

She looked at me.

"Are all these symptoms related to your marriage?" I asked.

I could feel the weight she carried on her shoulders as she shrugged. "When Stan is difficult and playing head games with me, my day will be horrible. He pushes for his way and is beyond stubborn. When he argues with me and then blames it all on me, I get worse. There was a day last week when I couldn't get out of bed."

"How does his arguing impact you?" I asked.

"I start the day with challenges," Debra said impatiently. "I can't handle any more stress, and relating with Stan does it to me. If I have only a little energy to start, struggling with him emotionally puts me on empty. Worse than empty!"

A Different Kind of Victim

Debra didn't arrive at my office complaining of NVS. She said she came to see me because she couldn't cope. In fact, she had never heard of NVS. She was anxious and worried about feeling sad and depressed. She had started reading about emotional abuse, and that triggered a bit of hope that it might not be all her. She thought she might be a victim.

Debra could feel herself slipping emotionally even though she was a strong Christian and felt loved by God. She wondered if she was being tested in some way by God, but this too was confusing to her. She felt the joy she had known previously slipping away and wondered what was happening to her.

I asked Debra to share more about her marriage.

"He's really self-centered," she said. "I think of him as a scheming teddy bear with brass knuckles. He can be loving at times, but he's always out for himself. He doesn't seem to notice that I'm dying, and that makes me furious."

She paused.

"I don't like the person I'm becoming. I have always been a loving and compassionate person. I believe in marriage, but I'm not sure I want to stay married to my husband."

Debra shared that I was the first person who seemed to understand what it might be like living with her husband. This was not surprising since many people have never heard of NVS. Thus, many women struggle with a syndrome that is not recognized or accurately diagnosed.

Not only have the victims rarely heard of this syndrome, but the people they seek help from—pastors, doctors, and therapists—know little about the syndrome as well. Most therapists have been trained to recognize depression or anxiety, common symptoms of someone struggling with NVS, but have little or no training in recognizing or treating NVS.

Because therapists are ill-equipped to deal with NVS, and friends and family have not even heard of this syndrome, the victim of NVS often goes unrecognized and unsupported and is left feeling helpless.

What Is Narcissistic Victim Syndrome (NVS)?

After taking a complete history, which is critically important, it was clear Debra was struggling with NVS. She had many of the common complaints consistent with NVS:

depression	weight loss or gain
fatigue/exhaustion	brain fog
insomnia	multiple physical complaints
anxiety	possibly suicidal
feeling empty	possibly dissociative
phobias	

These are some of the physiological and psychological complaints of women struggling with NVS. No two women have the same symptoms, which makes accurately assessing a woman more difficult. The common complaint, however, is feeling physically unwell—and is always associated with challenges in their marriage.

The victim of NVS must, of course, be in relationship with a narcissist. Additionally, as we have discussed, not all narcissists are created equal. Many seem like very nice guys, and therefore many women fear speaking up about this syndrome, which makes them feel crazy.

Post-Traumatic Stress Disorder (PTSD)

NVS is not the only possible problem facing the victim of narcissistic abuse. According to Christine Hammond's article "Identifying Victims of Narcissistic Abuse," many victims of narcissistic abuse struggle with post-traumatic stress disorder (PTSD), having possibly suffered one or more of the following:

- *Traumatic event.* Survivors have been exposed to actual or threatened death, serious injury, or sexual violence.

- *Intrusion or re-experiencing.* Victims experience intrusive thoughts or memories, nightmares, flashbacks, or psychological distress and reactions to reminders of the traumatic event.
- *Avoidant symptoms.* Victims may try to avoid memories of an event, including avoiding thoughts, feelings, memories, people, places, conversations, or situations connected to a traumatic event.
- *Negative alterations in mood or cognition.* Victims often experience a decline in mood or thought patterns after the event, including an inability to remember, negative beliefs, or expectations about one's self or the world. They also experience distorted thoughts about the cause or consequence of the event, fear, horror, anger, guilt, shame, diminished interest in activities, feeling detached, feeling estranged, or inability to experience happiness.
- *Increased arousal symptoms.* Victims may experience feelings of being "on edge," wary, and watching for further threats. Symptoms also include irritability, increased temper and anger, reckless, self-destructive behavior, difficulty falling or staying asleep, hypervigilance, difficulty concentrating, or being easily startled.
- *Symptoms lasting at least a month.* The symptoms must also seriously affect one's ability to function, and they can't be due to substance use, medical illness, or anything except the event itself.[1]

It is relatively easy to see how women like Debra are likely to suffer not only from NVS but also from PTSD. These women, in their troubled relationships, have often experienced myriad traumatic events that rocked their world. In fact, in many cases, daily life is filled with painful events.

In exploring Debra's history for possible PTSD, she shared, "I am always on edge with Stan. I never know if he is going to come home in a good or bad mood. If he's in a bad mood, nothing I do will be right."

"Has he ever threatened you in any way?" I asked.

"He has gotten in my face many times," she said. "He has never touched me, but he has let me know he could. He screams when he gets mad. He backs down when I start crying, but I know what he is capable of doing."

Debra shared again the pain she felt from giving up a career she loved.

"I just wasn't focusing the way I need to in order to run a classroom," she said. "I find myself thinking about what Stan was like the night before. I had been warned six months ago that people were noticing I wasn't functioning at a high enough level, so I gave my notice. Now I'm staying home, trying to get healthy."

Complex PTSD

As if these symptoms and struggles weren't bad enough for the victim of a narcissist, things often get much worse. Those who have been exposed to someone with a personality disorder, especially narcissistic personality disorder, can develop complex PTSD. Complex PTSD occurs when a victim experiences repeated trauma over which they have little or no control and from which there is perceived to be no real escape.

Most experts agree that victims suffering from complex PTSD share the following symptoms with PTSD: re-experiencing the past, having a sense of threat, and avoidance of the threatening situation. CPTSD differs from PTSD in that it has three additional symptoms:

- Emotional sensitivity and reduced ability to respond to situations in an emotionally appropriate manner
- Negative self-concept with feelings of worthlessness
- Interpersonal problems, marked by challenges in feeling close to others[2]

If you struggle with the concept of women having little control over their trauma, or their perceived inability to find real escape, consider Debra's situation.

Debra is only 40 years old. She was previously a dynamic teacher who worked hard to achieve her status and was beloved by parents and children. Because of repeated traumatic experiences, she now feels 20 years older than her age and is unable to work.

Debra can't just lie around in bed because of her constant fatigue and weariness—she has two teenage children who rely on her. Furthermore, she still loves her husband and desperately wants to hold on to her marriage. She believes in the sanctity of marriage and believes God has called her to love him, though at times she is intensely conflicted about those feelings. She dislikes him at times, creating a web of confusion.

Debra is a strong Christian and hates the thought of divorce and of harming her children. She has spent many years married, and her life is interwoven with her husband's.

The few people who know her well tell her she has a right to leave. Yet now that she is not working, she is more dependent upon her husband than before. She feels angry about her circumstances. Most people in her Christian circle don't fully understand her dilemma, but their general counsel is to "stay and pray."

Where is her clear path? What should she do?

Who's Listening?

You might think Debra could find plenty of support. Yet if you have been in her shoes, you know that is often not the case.

Those around her certainly acknowledge her pain and realize she is in distress, but where are the wounds? Who is the perpetrator? These are critical questions when it comes to finding support. The answers are not as easy to find as one might initially think.

"I feel like I'm screaming in the middle of a crowded room and no one can hear me," she said to me.

I sat silently, reflecting on what she said. I imagined her standing in the middle of a crowded room screaming and no one coming to her aid. What would it be like to be surrounded by people, cry out for help, but be ignored? The image is preposterous, right? Not necessarily. If no one really understands you, if they cannot fathom your experience, you are profoundly alone.

"Your words really impact me," I said to her. "I have been through some very painful times in my life, but I always had friends or family who supported me. In fact, I don't know how I could have survived my most painful experiences without dear friends caring for me. You describe being completely alone and without support or help."

"There is no one to help," she interrupted. "Even the professionals I've gone to don't really get it. They minimize my problems, or worse, they take my husband's side. When it's really bad, I get blamed for the problems. I'm truly alone and have to figure things out for myself."

The image lingered with me long after our counseling session. I considered some of the terrible experiences in my life and how I would have survived had I been alone. When I went through a painful divorce, I had a group of six men who prayed and stayed with me during the roughest of times. When I lost my mother, father, mother-in-law, and sister to cancer all within four years, I had family who loved me and understood my grief. What if I had been completely and utterly alone?

Women in narcissistic relationships feel alone because they are alone. Their mate cannot satisfy their emotional needs for empathic understanding and intimate connection. When seeking help, they are likely to meet with ineffective therapy, friends who don't understand, and pastors who will pray with them but do nothing else.

It's like screaming in the middle of a crowded room and no one coming to help.

Signs That You've Been Abused

NVS is real and it is debilitating, partly because of the abuse that precedes the syndrome and partly because of the lack of support and effective help for victims. Additionally, many people, including the victim, aren't sure what is going on. They are not sure what the matter is and what must be done for healing.

Victims of narcissistic abuse exhibit varied symptoms. Since the syndrome is not well known in clinical circles, the differing symptoms are not universally accepted. In many situations, the victims seek information on the Internet and from each other, and they inform the clinicians.

Kim Saeed, in her article "6 Strong Signs You Have Narcissistic

Abuse Syndrome," identified six signs that you are in relationship with a narcissist.

1. *You almost always feel alone.* Your mate may be with you physically, but you feel very detached from him because of his inability to connect in a healthy way. You'd love to have him connect emotionally, but he is incapable of really understanding your experience.
2. *You don't feel good enough.* Your partner rarely recognizes your accomplishments or shares in what matters most to you. He is completely bound up in his own world and accomplishments and is unable to focus on you, your feelings, and what matters most to you.
3. *You feel engulfed by the relationship.* Being excessively demanding, the narcissist takes over your life. He pushes for attention and admiration and steals your energy. You walk on eggshells trying to please him and keep him satisfied.
4. *You've begun to compromise your personal integrity and values.* You've begun tolerating bad behavior. You may have compromised your values and begun watching pornography with your husband, allowing him to use vulgar language with you, or tolerating other abusive behaviors you swore you would never tolerate.
5. *You feel unworthy due to your partner's name-calling.* Your mate has found it easier and easier to call you names when threatened or upset. Name-calling is abusive and belittling. Over time, the name-calling tears at your self-esteem and feelings for him.
6. *You are exhausted by the repeated cycles of hurt and rescue.* The narcissist causes you stress and anxiety and then does something to relieve that anxiety. He may give you the silent treatment or may completely shift and become

> charming and engaging again. He may threaten to leave you unless you change your behavior, and you comply because this is so scary.[3]

These signs offer a good summary of whether you are being abused. A clear review of your symptoms is possibly the best diagnosis of whether your mate is a narcissist or emotionally abusive. If you have any of the above symptoms, you can be sure something is wrong.

Understanding NVS

It is very difficult to fully understand NVS unless you have been there or are there. I have spoken to thousands of women who have been emotionally abused, but thankfully I have not experienced the abuse personally.

Lacking personal experience does not let anyone off the hook. When Scripture asks, "Am I my brother's keeper?" the appropriate response is a resounding yes. Jesus said, "I was hungry and you gave me something to eat, I was thirsty and you gave me something to drink, I was a stranger and you invited me in" (Matthew 25:35).

Friends, family, and professionals helping the victim of narcissistic abuse must understand the impact of the narcissist on the victim. We must understand the narcissist functions on the emotional level of a six-year-old—completely self-centered, personalizing anything that feels like criticism, and projecting all blame onto the victim. We must all circle around the victim to help mitigate the ongoing criticism, blame, and emotional chaos.

As you seek understanding, remember that interacting with the narcissist, especially when he feels threatened, will not bring about enlightenment. Rather, his response to anything threatening will be defensive and will lead to more chaos, confusion, and attempts to control you. When confronted, he feels threatened and is likely to either attack or withdraw. Growing and becoming healthier is *not* on his agenda—protecting himself is his primary objective.

Attempts to pull away will leave you feeling even more victimized. Lundy Bancroft mentions this in his book *Why Does He Do That?*

> If you...want to escape his abuse, you may find that you feel guilty toward him, despite his treatment of you, and have difficulty ending the relationship as a result. You may feel that because his life has been so hard, you are reluctant to add to his pain by abandoning him.[4]

This is not normal! You should not have to worry about saving him. You should not feel guilty if you choose to set some distance between the two of you so you can think straight. This is the roller coaster we've been talking about thus far in the book.

A Profound Loss of Self and Identity

All of these syndromes—NVS, PTSD, and complex PTSD—involve a profound loss of self and identity. What do I mean?

If you have been the victim of narcissistic and emotional abuse, you've spent a lot of time and energy trying to avoid his criticism. You've worked hard to avoid anger, resentment, and isolation. You have spent a lot of emotional energy trying to second-guess what he's thinking, feeling, and going to do, and all of this clouds your ability to care for an important person—you!

Many victims of NVS share the following sentiments:

"I've lost myself. I don't know who I am or what I like or what I want to do with my life. I've spent so much time focusing on him that I've lost myself. I'm just coping, hanging on."

Such statements suggest the woman is experiencing a profound loss of self. She's lost a critical part of herself, and this loss is disorienting. This basic aspect of her nature—her sense of self—has been shattered and must be rebuilt. Our core sense of self includes our ability to

think

feel

experience life

make decisions

discern what is best for us

impact others

determine our life's direction

dream and envision

choose new possibilities

Note the greatness of these aspects of our self. Created in the likeness of God, we are majestic creatures. We have the profound ability to think, evaluate, feel, and make decisions. We determine, in large part, the direction of our lives. We impact our well-being while also impacting every person we relate to, which is quite incredible.

Now imagine all of these abilities have disappeared for the victim of narcissistic abuse. Even though you are experiencing deep sadness, loss, confusion, and betrayal, you have lost something even more profound. Even though you've learned to cope, accommodate, and adapt to your situation, you have lost your self.

Tools for Recovery

Thankfully, there are skills and strategies for recovery from NVS and emotional abuse. We will focus on four power-packed tools to help you regain your emotional balance and set you on the path to healing.

Find Your Lost Heart

For many years you've been told you are stupid and oversensitive and your memory is faulty. You have been told you are overreactive and overly emotional and nothing about your core personhood is worth listening to or caring about. None of this is true!

God prizes women to the point of even being the last thing He created. He knew man could not survive well on his own and created woman to steward this planet together with him.

Moreover, God has used women throughout history, and we have poignant stories about Miriam, Jael, Rahab, Abigail, Ruth, Esther, and others who are woven into God's redemptive plan.

Naomi seemed to have done everything right in her life, yet she was met with one calamity after another. She lost her husband, sons, home, and friends. She had every reason to be despondent and discouraged. Did she really live faithfully only to have God turn His back on her? No!

As her story develops, we see God's plan unfold and her protection revealed through her daughter-in-law, Ruth. We see how she could not manage every detail of her life, but she trusted in the provision of God to save her. We see a woman who remained faithful, allowing God to show His love and care through Ruth. She learned a simple yet profound principle: Our best course of action is to trust God and remain faithful (Ruth 4:14-15).

You may need help in believing that principle again. You may have lost trust due to suffering from NVS. You may need help to see your thoughts are your own, your feelings are your own, and your dreams, desires, hopes, and longings are your own. You may need help believing that God cares about these things, that you are valued because you are a child of God.

The first part of finding your heart means admitting you are hurt. Your heart aches because of the abuse. You need to acknowledge that to yourself and have someone else sit with you and say, "That *did* hurt. You have been hurt deeply."

You need to connect to your heart again and begin to trust your perceptions and thoughts and feelings. This is where you get the footing to grasp what God thinks of you, to find healing, and to release the narcissist's control over you.

Untangle the Trauma Bond

There comes a point in time when it is less frightening to go along with what the narcissist says about you than it is for you to fight it or defend yourself against it. Believing the narcissist becomes an easier choice. The consequence, however, is to feel further hurt and trauma and loss of your sense of self.

Because you no longer trust your own judgment and are incredibly weary, you give in. You become even more emotionally dependent upon the narcissist to control the relationship, relying on him to stop the very harm he uses to control you. That dependency, also called a trauma bond, is cemented by moments of intermittent reward he throws in to keep you hooked. That intermittent reward—the brief euphoric hit— is powerful!

Subsequently, you will need to cultivate a growing sense of self-reliance to help you see that pattern of abuse and reward—the trauma bond. You must examine this cyclical pattern of reward and abuse, noting you have the ability to stop the cycle and untangle the trauma bond.

In addition to rediscovering your heart (what really matters to you) and untangling the trauma bond, here's a third important strategy.

Actively Disengage

This is hard to do. His behavior has, in many respects, destroyed your relationship. Since this is the case, you might think it would be simple to disengage. That is not true. The narcissist is an expert at hooking the victim, bringing her back into the brokenness to heap on even more brokenness, all the while blaming her and demanding she fix what he broke.

Many women find that a season of no contact helps them to think more clearly, regain their sense of self, and feel their own feelings once again. Whether this is a day, a week, or a month, it is the most effective way to silence the emotional chaos so you can think clearly, engage more wisely, and hold to your boundaries more consistently.

No contact *may* mean not responding to his attempts to contact you and reengage in the relationship. These are sometimes called *hoover maneuvers* because he is likely trying to suction you up (like a vacuum cleaner) into another cycle of abuse. These are his frightened attempts, born out of his own insecurity, to manipulate you back into the relationship. Learn to calm down your emotional system with self-soothing strategies (such as meditation, grounding, and changing your self-talk) to alleviate your panic so you can think more clearly and disengage from the narcissist's behavior.

Know Who You're Dealing With

Remember you are dealing with someone who thrives on power and control. He needs to be with someone he believes is of equal or lesser value than himself to feel important. If you challenge these perceptions directly, you will likely regret it. He is likely to respond vindictively.

This is not to say you must always dance around him and his issues. As I've said, beneath his tough exterior is a little boy who feels weak and insecure. Choose carefully when and how to confront him. Choose wisely on what you confront, ensuring it is a battle you can win.

Most important, work at changing you! As you become healthier, more centered, and sure of yourself, he will feel that change. He may not initially like it, but in time he may come to respect your boundaries more. As you change, he will likely change as well. As your sense of self becomes stronger, he will have a greater opportunity to change. At least he will begin to notice you are not going to be bullied and will know you mean what you are saying when you say no.

Celebrating Life Again

When you've been in an emotionally abusive relationship, it can be hard to open yourself to love again. You have been hurt, and that hurt has likely shattered your trust—both in yourself and others.

Being with a narcissist can leave you emotionally scarred and scared. You can learn to trust again after you understand what happened to you. What drew you to the narcissist in the first place? What kinds of tactics did he use, and how did you react? What has been the impact?

Whether you choose to stay or leave, do your inner work. Become stronger, clearer, and more resolved to regain your sense of self. Consider who God has created you to be and His faithfulness in your life. Reflect on the issues discussed in this chapter and how you have been impacted. Embrace the tools just discussed and practice them in your new life.

It is time to begin celebrating life again. You can learn to trust yourself, set boundaries on unhealthy actions, and treat yourself in more loving ways.

A Path Forward

You have undoubtedly learned a lot by now. Are you becoming stronger? Do you feel more courageous and willing to make changes to save your life? You have one life to save, and that is your own.

We are now moving forward and examining a central aspect of this book—emotional abuse and its many faces. In learning what emotional abuse looks like, you will be empowered to keep yourself safe and grow beyond the abuse.

Part 2

Emotional Abuse

6

The Many Faces of Emotional Abuse

Do not think of yourself more highly than you ought.

ROMANS 12:3

Jim is a nice guy. I really like him. He is ambitious, having carved out a very successful career at General Motors. He has been a loyal member of the GM team for nearly 30 years, garnering the respect of many.

Affable and caring, Jim didn't seem to fit the mold of the narcissistic men I was accustomed to seeing. When interacting with me, he was friendly, open, and excited about the next phase of his life.

Jim was nearing retirement. His exit plan was squarely in place, his nest egg was impressive, and he was eyeing ways he could give more time and expertise to his church and community.

Jim proudly talked about his three grown children, successful and solid Christians with spouses and children. He had helped his children with college tuition and down payments on their first homes. He was not boastful of the legacy he would leave behind.

From the outside, Jim appeared to be living the dream. And he was—with one exception. He and his wife, Jackie, had a stormy relationship, and it had been this way for the past ten years.

"Well, Jackie and I live with constant tension," he sheepishly admitted. "I can't seem to please her, and I know I'm not happy with her. She always seems angry with me, and I must admit being resentful of her. I don't know what I'm doing wrong, but she insisted I work with you."

"Why did she ask you to work with me, Jim?" I asked.

"I'm not really sure," he said cautiously. "You'll have to ask her. I'm sure she'll tell you."

"But I'd like to know why you think she asked you to work with me."

"She thinks I'm controlling and angry," he said. "I think she's angrier than me. I'm angry that she is angry."

Jackie offered a very different story.

"Please don't be fooled," she said anxiously. "You're our fourth counselor, including pastors, and they all think Jim is a saint. Of course, he doesn't show his hostile side to them. I'm the only one who sees that. He can be downright mean. If things don't go his way, he'll pull away from me. He twists what I say and turns it back on me. Heaven forbid I dare criticize him."

"Hasn't anyone held him accountable for these actions?" I asked incredulously.

"No one sees it," she said. "He looks good, acts good, and fools everyone. I don't stand a chance. Please don't let him fool you too."

Jackie was another woman anxiously hoping I wouldn't be fooled, as so many others have also hoped.

He Seems So Innocent

With few people really listening to their pain, and their mate having a perfect presentation to others, it is no wonder abused women are feeling unheard.

"He appears so innocent," I frequently hear. In the past ten years of my practice, I've worked with well over 4000 couples, and in most of those, the men have had narcissistic and emotional abuse issues. The women, without exception, said the behavior their husband displays to others appears so charming, yet in private is phenomenally debilitating—to the point of creating physical symptoms in the women.

How is this possible? How can men like Jim seem so nice, be so kind to so many people, and yet be labeled emotionally abusive? Let's consider these possibilities.

First, *emotional abuse is subtle.* Men like Jim may be part charming, part cunning, and part oppressive. Their shadow side, unseen by many, can include behaviors such as pouting, stonewalling, and shifting the focus. At first glance, these emotionally abusive behaviors can seem innocuous.

You might be thinking, "Pouting is emotionally abusive?" Yes. Pouting, or passive-aggressive silence, done again and again, will create chaos in a relationship. Stonewalling—refusing to talk about an issue—will do the same. Add them together and you've got real trouble.

Second, *we are just now starting to recognize emotional abuse.* Several years ago we would never have called these behaviors abusive. They were either not labeled as troubling or were labeled merely as pet peeves. They may have been lumped into a category of "men being men." But no, they are not just troubling behaviors. They are abusive behaviors, stealing a woman's sense of self.

Third, *our society wants to deny emotional abuse.* Not only do we fail to recognize or call out emotional abuse, but worse, we deny it when it blatantly occurs. Unlike with physical violence, with a black eye or a broken arm, there are no community resources available when emotional violence occurs.

Finally, *very few trained clinicians are dealing with these issues.* Emotional abuse still receives little attention in therapy training programs. Domestic violence is still treated as acts of overt violence, while many churches and communities resist talking openly about covert emotional abuse.

So you can see why so many women feel alone, abandoned, and voiceless. You can understand why women such as Jackie swirl in feelings of confusion, wondering if they are imagining a problem where none exists.

Fooled

Jackie is profoundly alone. In a world just beginning to listen to complaints of emotional abuse, she screams to be heard, all the while feeling unheard.

The many faces of emotional abuse have indeed fooled a lot of people. Most don't recognize these faces. They are unfamiliar.

Jackie shared her story.

"I tell people in my Bible study about Jim withdrawing from me for days when he gets mad, and they tell me they will pray for me. I tell them he glares at me when I confront him about something small, and they tell me things will work out. I want to scream. I don't share much with them anymore."

"Most people don't consider these actions abusive," I shared. "When you tell people about Jim abandoning you emotionally, many see that behavior as simply childish, not abusive. When you share about him glaring at you, they don't fully appreciate the impact his intimidation has on your emotional well-being."

"Try living with it every day," she said piercingly.

"Yes, that is what really makes it emotional abuse," I said. "Those behaviors are really harmful to you. Anyone would be wounded by those behaviors."

Jackie seemed relieved to hear me say that. Few have given her that comfort and validation.

Bear in mind that Jim has a brighter side as well. Contrast his darker behaviors with his healthier side. Remember he makes a fantastic salary at GM and is generous with his wife, children, church, and community. He is not a bad man. No one experiences the weight of his emotional abuse except his wife.

This is one of any victim's worst fears—that their mate's behavior will fool others. Self-doubt is particularly perplexing. They fear they may be exaggerating his behavior and overreacting. They also fear friends and family will be fooled and they will be cast in a bad light (scapegoating)—another covert emotionally abusive tactic where the man looks good and the woman looks bad.

Though many will be fooled, failing to see his abusive side, make no mistake about the gravity of his actions. Emotional deprivation is brutal. Though many will never see them, his glares are not innocuous. His glares are threatening. His glares create emotional instability and distance. His glares reveal a hardened heart and give rise to other emotionally abusive, egregious actions.

Signs of Emotional Abuse

Though many will be fooled, you can be informed. You can be an individual who understands emotional abuse and the impact it has had on your life. Having this knowledge, you are empowered to be a stronger and fuller human being.

One of the confusing aspects of emotional abuse is that it is not easy to recognize. Taking one incident at a time, emotional abuse may be mistaken for an act of irresponsibility or immaturity—a harsh word here, a scolding look there.

It is all of that, but added together it's so much more.

It is imperative to understand that emotional abuse is not a singular action, but rather a pattern of actions. Emotional abuse is not one glare or angry outburst, but rather a pattern of glares, outbursts, neglect, and hurtful behaviors. It is not an occasional sharp word spoken, but rather a pattern of hurtful, damaging words spoken consistently. Emotional abuse is a plethora of behaviors, comments, and attitudes that create a profound lack of safety for the victim.

The abusive behaviors develop into patterns or cycles. If there is a rare apology, remorse is fleeting, change does not occur, and the victim feels no safer.

With this in mind, let's learn more about what exactly constitutes emotional abuse.

Emotional abuse is defined as any coercive and threatening behavior or action used to control or manipulate how another will think or behave. These actions are strategically used to force another into thinking what is acceptable or not acceptable according to the abusive individual.

Focus on the Family has taken this position: "Emotional abuse is any nonphysical behavior or attitude that controls, intimidates, subjugates, demeans, punishes or isolates another person by degradation, humiliation or fear."[1]

What are some ways this is done?

1. *Hypercriticism.* Can you imagine living with constant criticism? Can you imagine living with someone who is

never satisfied with your actions? Emotional abuse occurs when one lives with constant criticism.

2. *Humiliation.* Living with criticism is one thing, but it's quite another to feel another's contempt or ridicule. "Why did you do it that way?" "Why would you ever do that?" Humiliation degrades another and steals their sense of well-being.

3. *Refusing to communicate.* Many women have told me they would rather be hit than ignored. They hate the emotional neglect and isolation that comes from his refusal to communicate when angry. Being ignored, given the cold shoulder, is brutal.

4. *Sarcasm or provocation.* The occasional provocative word can be tolerated and dealt with in the relationship. A sarcastic comment bites. A provocative word hurts. When these words are continually woven into the fabric of the relationship, trust and safety are quickly eroded.

5. *Withholding affection.* Jackie shared the impact of Jim withholding affection from her. "He sucks the life out of me not only by what he says but by what he does. He withholds affection and emotional connection. He stopped coming close years ago, and it kills me. He knows it hurts and yet keeps doing it."

6. *Excessive jealousy.* How do you fight against the man who believes you are cheating on him when that is the furthest thing from your mind? How do you reassure a man of your faithfulness when you may question his? Excessive jealousy, on either partner's side, is very hurtful, eroding trust and emotional safety.

7. *Isolation from friends and family.* Slowly but surely he isolates you from friends and family. He finds something wrong with every one of your friends and believes your

family has it out for him. Subsequently, his criticism leads to you giving up and giving in, separating you from your friends and family. The impact, of course, is devastating and unhealthy.

8. *Control of money, decisions, and communication.* The final act of insecure power is that of control. He controls and dominates your use of money, the decisions you make, and the ways you do or don't communicate. He believes he is superior and shows it.

These emotionally abusive behaviors are devastating to your self-esteem. They cause you to live in fear and isolation. They tear at the fabric of your personhood and the integrity of your relationship with him. They erode your sacred sense of self. They are symbols of his weak ego and need for power and control, and they can leave you feeling small and insecure.

Covert Emotional Abuse

Overt abuse often includes yelling, shoving, and physical acts of harm. *Covert* emotional abuse, however, doesn't include physical acts of violence, though the threat of violence may loom in the shadows. The emotional abuser may make it clear that harm can come to you if you don't change your behavior to meet his expectations.

But typically, covert abuse is passive abuse. No less damaging than overt abuse, covert abuse may involve gaslighting—attempting to alter your perceptions and reality to match his intended goals. He may rewrite history or strongly challenge your viewpoint to meet his needs. Covert abuse may involve hiding money and then accusing you of making things up, causing you to wonder if you are seeing the situation clearly.

Covert emotional abuse makes you feel crazy. Any complaints you have are turned back on you (blame shifting). Intolerant of criticism, he is easily angered. Challenges to his power are met with defensiveness and attacks on you.

While not overtly physically dangerous, his manipulations certainly have an impact on your emotional and physical well-being. We are mind-body creatures, so it is no surprise that constant tension steals our sense of well-being. Your body will likely begin to feel the toll of his tension-creating actions.

Covert emotional abuse involves him lying to protect himself. He may weave stories that make him look innocent, leaving you questioning your sanity. He dismisses you, "forgetting" what is important to you, and criticizes you for being critical of him.

In one particularly telling blog post titled "Subtle Signs You're Being Manipulated by a Covert Abuser," Lisa Arends wrote that covert abuse is sneaky. She noted that her ex-husband came from a troubled family, and that should have been her first warning sign. He never voiced displeasure. He got along with many people but had few close friends. He was a "storyteller" who could blend plausible fiction with reality.

She noted, "It doesn't leave a bruise on your cheek. Or cut you down with scathing words. Or even obviously isolate you from others. Instead, it wisps in slowly through tiny cracks...The smoke builds until you no longer remember what it is like to see clearly and your head is filled more with the thoughts of your abuser than your own."[2]

Covert abuse is subtle and manipulative—but not innocent. Whether perpetrated consciously or a chronic, unhealthy pattern of relating, these actions are devastating.

Scapegoating and Playing the Victim

There are many covert emotional abuse tactics, but there are two I especially want to examine. They are both particularly devious and particularly powerful.

Scapegoating

The concept comes from the Old Testament, where a goat is designated to be led away into the wilderness, bearing the sins of the community. For our purposes, a person is selected as a scapegoat (the emotionally abused woman), bearing the brunt of a problem belonging to the emotional abuser.

Jackie is Jim's scapegoat. The process is subtle and debilitating. They attend church together, and he is active in the community. In each venue, he appears outgoing, friendly, and marked with integrity. Any efforts Jackie has made to bring light to his harmful actions have been largely ignored. She is seen as whiny, not appreciating how good she's got it.

At first this scene may seem innocuous, but it is anything but that. The horrific damage of this situation is that Jim enjoys the favor of the community while Jackie suffers alone and is viewed in a negative light. To make matters worse, he does nothing to set the record straight, enabling the negative views—and that is the terrible power of scapegoating.

Said another way, scapegoating is the process of allowing a wrong, negative perception to stand uncontested. When the perpetrator allows his mate to sustain unwarranted criticism, he engages in scapegoating. He actively scapegoats her when he fails to correct a negative perception, enjoying favor while his wife experiences the harm of a wrong impression or reputation.

Can you see it? Perhaps not at first. It has taken me years to appreciate the power of scapegoating and the incredible damage it does to the victim. This is the most powerful aspect of covert emotional abuse.

Playing the Victim

In this instance the perpetrator turns the tables on the real victim.

"Whenever I criticize him in the slightest, he turns things back onto me. He says things like, 'I can never please you,' or 'You're never going to stop complaining.' This makes me feel crazy and makes me stop and worry about my actions."

Playing the victim is a most debilitating tactic because it stops her from sharing any concerns and it causes her to wonder about her own actions. Maybe he *is* being treated unfairly. Maybe she *is* being too critical. Maybe he really *can't* do enough to satisfy her, strongly suggesting her standards are way out of line.

As with all other defenses, these emotionally abusive tactics create an environment where she is subtly harmed and incredibly unsafe. His actions stop her from asking for change, and they create uncertainty and confusion. She experiences his blame, creating self-doubt and erosion of her self-esteem. This is why we call these actions crazy making.

A Problem of Self-Protection

Whether conscious or subconscious, one thing is clear—covert emotional abuse is designed to protect the abuser and place the innocent victim in danger. Much narcissistic and emotional abuse is a defensive maneuver designed to protect the abuser.

Protect him from what?

The emotional abusers' defenses are all crafted to protect them from feeling healthy shame and vulnerability. They hate feeling bad and would rather *you* feel hurt and wounded. Victims sense they are allowed to feel harm while the abusers protect themselves. This is excruciating.

This goes against how we were created. God placed within us a conscience so we could know right from wrong, good from evil. We were designed by God to feel sorrow for wrongful actions. This rightful way of functioning, however, has gone awry for the emotional abuser, who avoids healthy shame and remorse with his many defensive mechanisms.

Let's peer again into Jackie's life.

Jackie shared on one particular Sunday afternoon that she tentatively approached Jim about taking a day off from football and spending it with her. She was soft and kind in her delivery. What she got back was a blast.

"I only take one day off a week, and I'd like to spend it watching football. Is that too much to ask? Don't try to guilt-trip me for doing something for myself. I'll spend it with you, but I sure don't know why I can't do something for myself once in a while."

What happened? Why was her request met with a defensive blast from Jim? Was Jackie harsher than she is admitting? Did she guilt-trip him into spending time with her? Does she guilt-trip him when he does *anything* for himself? Unlikely.

I'm offering a more plausible explanation. Jim felt inadequate when Jackie asked him to spend time with her. Rather than feeling inadequate, he projected his inadequate feelings onto her. He overreacted and blamed her for things she had not done. His outburst was one of his many ways of protecting himself, causing emotional chaos in the process.

Emotional abuse is largely a pattern of behaviors used to protect the abuser from painful feelings. As you have read, emotionally abusive men are broken and hurting and often emotionally underdeveloped. Like little boys, they act out their feelings rather than expressing them effectively.

Imagine how the above scene could have been handled effectively. What if Jim had said, "Honey, I know I don't spend enough time with you. How about if I watch just one football game and we spend the rest of the day doing something together? Could that work for you?"

There. Problem solved. Nobody gets their feelings hurt, and everyone wins.

Denial

If Jim would have approached his wife with vulnerability, the situation would have gone smoothly. All he had to do was admit to wrongdoing, and life would likely have moved forward.

There's the crucial hitch. In this win-win scenario, Jim admits to being less than perfect. He is vulnerable and kind. He takes note of her feelings. He admits that he has failed—something emotionally abusive men don't do.

A man in denial can't admit his weaknesses, and this is a huge issue. Remember, he doesn't want to feel healthy shame, so he goes to great lengths to avoid those painful feelings. Subsequently, his reactions and defenses become the issue rather than her pain.

Denial—avoidance of feeling healthy shame—is a powerful enemy of healthy marriages. Denial keeps Jim from facing his weaknesses and working with Jackie on solutions that will work for both of them. Denial keeps him in self-protection mode. It keeps him always pushing Jackie away and finding fault in her rather than himself.

Denial is the highest form of self-protection, and it works—but it creates abject chaos in the process. Blaming Jackie keeps the onus off him. Gaslighting so that she questions herself keeps her from finding fault with him. Ranting and raving keeps her on her toes so that she is never too critical of him.

Jim's actions work, but with a huge price tag—intimacy, trust, and connection are lost. Additionally, he remains stuck in his immaturity.

Her Denial Too

Jackie simply wants a connection to Jim. She is not out to make him the bad guy. She wants him to do what everyone wants their mate to do—to take responsibility for his actions so they can effectively solve problems and grow together.

Moreover, she wants him to make reparative actions for his wrongdoing so they can remain connected. This, however, takes emotional honesty, which is something he doesn't possess.

Jackie also wants to be accepted. She walks on eggshells so she won't take the brunt of his criticism, victim stance, and blame shifting. Though tempted at times to explode at Jim, she stuffs her feelings in an attempt to save their marriage.

Sadly, Jackie has not grappled with, or come to accept, the fact that she will not receive Jim's acceptance the way their relationship is working. She has not reconciled herself with the fact that Jim is broken, wounded, and hurting and cannot give the acceptance she deserves and needs. She has not faced the fact that change will only come with significant intervention.

Just as Jim is in denial, Jackie is in denial as well. She lives with anxiety and fear because she hopes beyond hope that Jim will wake up one day and realize what he's doing. Sadly, this is magical thinking. This cannot happen without an intervention. She cannot receive something he cannot now give. She cannot extract from him something he is ill-equipped to give. She must ready herself for the intervention that leads to the possibility of change.

Are you at the point of an intervention? Are you ready to break out of denial and into the possibility of real change? If you are tired of living the way you've been living and desperately want change, you may be ready to insist upon change.

Signs of Times for Change

Before Jackie can be ready for change, she must come out of denial. She must face her signs of distress. The truth certainly will set us free, but not before it scares the daylights out of us. We all must know when we are in emotional trouble.

How can you know when you are being emotionally abused?

Abby Rodman, in a wonderful article titled "You're Not Going Crazy: 5 Sure Signs You're Being Emotionally Abused," cited five ways to recognize if you are being emotionally abused.

1. *You receive discouragement rather than support.* Look for patterns. Do you receive more discouragement than encouragement and support? This is a danger sign.

2. *You receive criticism rather than admiration.* Are you constantly criticized? Remember that ongoing criticism erodes self-esteem and positive connection. Criticism tears down one's emotional well-being. This is a serious danger sign.

3. *You receive indifference rather than empathy.* Does he tune in and attend to your joys and sorrows? If not, you're in trouble. Accurate empathy heals and brings connection, while indifference creates disconnection.

4. *You live in chaos rather than balance.* Does he bring emotional stability to the relationship? Life should be lived in peacefulness. Chaos creates tension and anxiety and is a particularly concerning danger sign.

5. *He assigns blame rather than taking responsibility.* Relationships need ongoing reparative work. Couples must be well equipped to say "I'm sorry" and then take restorative action. Our sorrow should lead to change and repair. This is a strong danger sign.[3]

Those are certainly five quick ways to determine if it is time for change in the way you relate to each other. These signs are indicators that your marriage may be fraught with emotional abuse.

The Power of Intervention

What should you do if you see your life in these many faces of emotional abuse? What should you do if you noted a number of danger signs in your relationship?

It is up to you to take action. You don't have to settle for abuse, nor do you have to go to the other extreme of giving up on your relationship. Rather, there is power in intervention.

What exactly is an intervention?

First, here is what intervention is not. Intervention is not fighting fire with fire. In other words, it's not becoming angry and sarcastic with him. It's not developing a rebellious and resentful attitude. This harms you far more than it impacts him.

Intervention is also not becoming reactive. It is not being impulsive and making decisions likely to hurt everyone. An intervention is not easy, and it takes great courage.

Intervention, in simplest terms, is making decisions to stop harmful actions. Intervention is refusing to tolerate harmful behavior, making strong decisions to manage your life more effectively. Perhaps an example will help.

Jackie worked with me on constructing an intervention for Jim's hostility. I asked her about the exact nature of his hostility so we could more effectively design an intervention.

"He gets short with me when he feels impatient. When things don't go the way he wants, he criticizes me."

"Okay," I said. "How about this? Let him know you will no longer tolerate his criticism. Let him know you will listen to his concerns only when he brings them to you respectfully."

"He'll probably simply ignore me," she said.

"Very possibly, at least at first," I said. "But if you practice this consistently, regardless of where or when it happens, I'm sure you will have an impact. In fact, if it happens in public, let him know you wish to be taken home immediately. Then let him know you expect an apology."

"I don't think he will go for this," she said softly.

"He probably won't at first," I said. "Perhaps not ever. But you will have done all you can to bring about change. He will know when he has offended you, and he'll have a clear choice to change or not."

"One final thought," I added. "Remember that you are changing you, not him. You are managing your behavior. Your success hinges on how you have accomplished your goals, not whether he changes."

Jackie liked that concept.

Accountability

Intervention is powerful, but it must be coupled with another important step—accountability. I am surprised to notice how few couples weave accountability into their relationship.

Change rarely occurs easily. Stopping emotional abuse is like stopping a moving freight train. Emotionally abusive men have practiced unhealthy patterns of behavior for years, so change will not come easily. But it can happen.

Here's what I mean by accountability. You must establish a clear boundary—what you will and will not tolerate—and then manage that boundary effectively.

I'll share an example from my life. Some time ago my wife, Christie, told me she felt unsafe with my driving, asking me to use my blinkers and to come to a full stop at stop signs.

I must admit I didn't take kindly to her request. I felt restricted and confused. Why did she need me to use my blinkers at every turn? Was she trying to control me? Maybe, but that didn't make sense. She had no need to be controlling. But I didn't want to accept that she didn't feel safe with my driving.

Of course, she was right to tell me about her fears, regardless of my experiencing a bit of restriction. True empathy required me to stop playing the victim, feel her feelings, and honor her request, which I have done (mostly).

Enter accountability. A short time ago she reminded me of my agreement to attend to her feelings. She reminded me that I could choose to have her ride with me and feel safe, or we could drive separately. Point made! Her accountability was a gift and brought about lasting change.

The Path Forward

Emotional abuse, whether overt or covert, is powerfully damaging. For your health, it must stop. When you are connected to someone covertly manipulative and silently and secretly devious, you are being victimized. You deserve a life of safety, protection, and honor.

Understanding the emotionally abusive tactics in this chapter will help you take decisive steps to stand against them. Knowledge is power. Are you ready for an intervention? Are you prepared to hold your man accountable for depth change? You are worthy of such change.

The covert emotionally abusive tactics mentioned in this chapter are not our only focus. Let's now move forward and learn about secondary emotional abuse.

7

Enabling as Secondary Abuse

The only thing necessary for evil to triumph
is for good men to do nothing.

EDMUND BURKE

Gina spends most days alone in a small, one-bedroom apartment. What would make this bright, 47-year-old mother of three grown children choose to live alone, well below her customary standard of living?

"My husband was so abusive I simply couldn't stay any longer," she told me. "It's the hardest decision I've ever made. He's still in our family home because he refused to leave. I told him that if he wasn't going to leave, I was. I was not going to live under his domination any longer. I was slowly dying."

Gina was angry.

"Our kids think I'm overreacting and see their dad as the victim, and I don't really care. They will figure it out for themselves someday."

"What happened to bring you to this point?" I asked.

"I couldn't take it anymore," she said. "Karl is so incredibly rigid. He hasn't apologized for one thing in our entire marriage. Nothing I ever did was ever good enough. I was afraid I was losing my mind."

"How do you feel now?" I asked.

"Sad," she said, looking away. "My kids blame me. They think I should go back home, but I can't. They don't really see what he's done, and he sure isn't going to explain it to them. He's filling the kids' heads with garbage about me. He complains about his life and makes it sound like I'm crazy."

She paused.

"Why do you say that?" I asked.

"He doesn't take responsibility for any of this," she said. "He's in denial about it all. He's told all our friends and family some story, like 'I wasn't the husband I should have been,' but no more. He doesn't tell them about his perfectionism. He doesn't tell them that he had me on a budget for 20 years. He doesn't tell them about all the rules he made up. He acts like he's the victim. He's proud of himself for admitting that much. 'Poor me.'"

"What do your friends and family think?" I asked.

"They've seen some of what he does, but not much," she said. "They aren't going to confront him. I think they're afraid to stick their noses into our lives. Our friends don't say anything, his family supports him, and our church family doesn't want to get involved. Our pastor says he's praying for us."

"What you're describing is known as *secondary abuse*, Gina," I said. "Secondary abuse is when others stand by and allow you to be abused. Secondary abuse is when pastors, therapists, friends, and family refuse to take a stand against abuse, leaving the victim to fend for herself."

"Well, it's horrible," she said. "I feel more alone now than when I was with my husband. I'm really starting to doubt myself."

A New Kind of Alone

Gina is experiencing a new kind of alone and a new kind of abuse. Not only must she recover from the years of emotional abuse, she must do it largely alone—at least until she finds support. When family and friends stand by and watch abuse happening without taking a stand, they enable abuse.

These are strong words. You may have to sit back and reflect on this. You may even disagree with me. But watching a friend or loved one take the blame for something that is not their responsibility is wrong—and it is abusive. That is what this chapter is about—enabling as a form of abuse.

Gina shared how she felt painfully alone in her marriage.

Surrounding herself with her children and their activities had insulated her from some of the emotional abuse from her businessman husband. Deep down, however, she knew she felt an ache in her heart.

"When our youngest child left home, I couldn't hold it together any longer," she shared. "Karl ran our home like he ran his real estate company. He ordered me around and expected everything to be the way he wanted it to be."

"How is he with the kids?" I asked.

She paused.

"The kids love their father," she said. "He gives them anything they want. But he's also tough on them. They were afraid of him and did whatever he demanded of them while they were growing up."

"And how was he with your parenting?" I asked.

"He has always undermined my authority with them, and I pretty much gave up trying to be the type of mother I wanted to be. I became a Stepford wife. I felt like a robot doing exactly what he wanted me to do. I've felt so painfully alone in my marriage, and now I'm a new kind of alone. Maybe it's good though. Maybe now I can rediscover who I was really made to be, not just who he defined me to be."

"You waited until your children were grown," I observed.

"My children mean everything to me," she said. "I just didn't want to break up the family. They didn't see much of what was going on, or at least they don't act like they saw it. Maybe they know more than I think. I know my friends and church family don't see it. I worked pretty hard to hide it. Everyone is in massive denial."

Betrayal

Betrayal is particularly painful. It's often a part of the enabling process and thus a part of abuse. When you are in emotional pain and others refuse to acknowledge it, you feel incredibly alone and betrayed.

To say, "I feel betrayed" may be hard for you. It may be hard to even acknowledge this is one of your feelings. Who wants to look at their mate, family, and friends and acknowledge they've been betrayed?

No one.

We expect loyalty from those we care about. We expect them to stand by us in good times and in bad. When times are tough, we really expect family and friends to come to our rescue. When they don't, we feel a deep sense of violation and betrayal.

You might be tempted to let people off the hook. "They're doing the best they can," you think. "They don't want to choose sides and are in a difficult spot."

Perhaps it's true. Yet there comes a time when it is critical to take a stand. When it comes to mistreatment, it's important to stand by friends or family. To fail to do so is betrayal—and that causes deep pain and is a form of secondary abuse.

As much as we might not want to, we must acknowledge betrayal. When using the word "betrayal," most think of a major incident, such as an affair. Mira Kirshenbaum, in her book *I Love You, but I Don't Trust You*, describes betrayal:

> You have an expectation of someone—a normal, reasonable expectation—and the other person violates it... Betrayal is a kind of reliability breakdown...Which is worse, one big betrayal or a seemingly endless series of little betrayals? If you were about to say one big betrayal and then hesitated, good for you. Of course anything can happen with any two people. But in general, relationships have an easier time dealing with one big betrayal than an endless series of little ones.[1]

Secondary abuse is about a series of betrayals. It is about friends who choose to believe you are more the perpetrator than the victim. It is about family who chooses to see you as more the instigator of trouble than the victim of it. Secondary abuse is about a pastor and church body who don't want to hear about emotional abuse because it's uncomfortable for them and insist you haven't given him enough of a chance.

This all equates to a massive, ongoing series of betrayals.

Turning Away

Before we become too critical of all these people who turn away from the victim of emotional abuse, let's try to understand what is going on.

Why would friends turn away from friends? Why might family turn away from family? Why might a church body turn away from one of their members? Again, the answer is not simple.

Dr. Gregory Jantz helps us understand what might be happening. Emotional abuse is all around us and yet may be so common it is ignored. Dr. Jantz, author of "Have We Learned to Ignore Emotional Abuse?" thinks part of the answer lies in the commonality of emotional abuse.

> Being part of the cultural, social, and personal landscape, it has come to be ignored. As long as anyone can remember, Grandpa talked that way to Dad, who talked that way to Junior, who in turn talks that way to his own kids.[2]

Jantz goes on to illustrate the phenomenon of so many people turning their heads and ignoring emotional abuse, which leads to secondary abuse. Or perhaps worse, not turning their heads and allowing emotional abuse to happen under their noses. He points out that television has always promoted emotional abuse with characters like Archie Bunker from *All in the Family*, Al Bundy in *Married with Children*, and Homer Simpson in *The Simpsons*—all of whom were foul-tempered and sarcastic and exhibited verbal put-downs.

Archie, Al, and Homer have all been popular and have made us laugh, albeit inappropriately. We emotionally turned away from the emotional abuse. We stood by as the women and children in these scenes suffered from primary and secondary abuse.

Consider that each time we laugh, turn away from, ignore, or stand by idly, we participate in the secondary abuse. Each time we watch, we forget someone is being harmed, someone is being emotionally abused.

Enabling

Turning away at the sight of discomfort is nothing new. Throughout history we have turned our heads and pretended not to see horror. Whether it has been on a global scale (the Holocaust and ongoing genocides), our national level (slavery and continuing racism), or within our communities (commercially sanctioned addictions), we know about enabling.

Enabling is not a new concept. When used in a positive connotation it can mean helping someone achieve what they want to accomplish. Enabling can be empowering. When used regarding abuse, of course, it's not positive.

Enabling dysfunctional behavior is very detrimental, occurring when third parties take responsibility for someone's problems or when others make excuses or accommodations for a person's harmful behavior.

At first glance, enabling may seem benign, but it is anything but that. Here are just a few of its serious ramifications worth considering.

1. *Someone else often takes responsibility for the problem.* The guilty individual is spared from taking full responsibility for their behavior. In fact, the innocent person often takes the blame.

2. *Accommodations and excuses are made for the dysfunctional behavior.* The dysfunctional behavior (abuse) is strengthened when it's allowed to continue and even be reinforced. Change cannot occur where there is enabling.

3. *The guilty person then doesn't have to take responsibility for their troubling behavior.* Since the guilty person's behavior (abuse) is enabled, they don't have to take responsibility for it and change. Without taking responsibility, change cannot occur. What is not confronted is rarely owned, and what you don't own and take full responsibility for, you don't change.

4. *From a broader perspective, the troubling behavior leads to greater societal problems.* The problem, multiplied, becomes a larger issue. Society is harmed when troubling behavior (abuse) is allowed to continue.

Let's now take a closer look at what happens when abuse is enabled.

Enabling Abuse

I make no apologies if at this point you are starting to become uncomfortable. It's okay. We've all participated in secondary abuse to the extent that we've not intervened for a victim. It was easier to go along with the crowd than to stand up for the real victim.

It's easy to enable abuse. It's easy to stand by and act as if we don't see what is going on, or perhaps we are so deep in our own denial that we really don't see what is happening.

A short time ago my wife and I were traveling and came upon a young couple who were obviously fighting. The angry man was standing over the young woman, yelling at her. She cupped her head and was sobbing.

I slowed for the briefest of moments, feeling uneasy and awkward. I felt sorry for the young woman but did nothing. I was angry with the man but did nothing. After my momentary pause, I kept walking.

"It's not my business," I thought. "Maybe it's not as bad as it looks. Maybe this is a rare and unfortunate moment, and they will be back to normal soon. Regardless, it's not my business."

Certainly you've been in similar circumstances. You've overheard a man yelling at a woman and have done nothing. You've stood by instead of intervening, because that's what we do. As a result, you and I have allowed victims to suffer.

Did I do the right or wrong thing on that street that day? Should I have asked if she needed help? When you faced similar circumstances, should you have intervened?

These kinds of decisions are not easy to make. I don't know that I would do anything different if I were to happen upon a similar situation today. Stepping into a volatile situation of any kind places us in harm's way. Most often we'd rather pretend nothing bad is happening and go on with our lives.

Let's reconsider Gina's situation.

She raised a family in an abusive home. She held it together. Once the children were gone, she made a decision to change her life. She had cultivated a quiet yet powerful conviction of right and wrong that would urge her into her new life.

Now she is alone, working every day and trying to recover from years of abuse. No one asks how bad it was to live with her abusive husband. No one probes for details on why she left. The circle of people who enabled her abuse is wide and deep. She tries not to be resentful toward those who could have helped, but she doesn't always win that battle.

Few reach out to her. Few ask what happened. Few want to get their hands dirty by standing up for what is right. This is the power and impact of enabling secondary abuse.

Scapegoating and Triangulation

I spoke about scapegoating in the last chapter, but the topic deserves far more attention. Remember that scapegoating occurs when the abuser allows the abused to have the negative reputation the abuser deserves. Scapegoating occurs when he points the blame at her and then refuses to take responsibility while she suffers. Scapegoating occurs when the perpetrator stands by, soaking up positive impressions, and encourages the victim to be seen as the troublemaker.

The process of scapegoating occurs through the power of *triangulation*, the process where one person experiences conflict with another but goes to a third person to discuss the problem, forming a triangle. Gossip is the fuel that keeps the triangulation and scapegoating alive.

Scapegoating and triangulation are always destructive. Triangulation often involves playing one person against another, creating even more hard feelings. Scapegoating and triangulation occur when the perpetrator goes to others and plays the victim. The real victim is talked about negatively and cast in the darkest light. The perpetrator gathers people on his side while the victim suffers secondary abuse. This is clearly not what Jesus intended.

> Therefore, if you are offering your gift at the altar and there remember that your brother or sister has something against you, leave your gift there in front of the altar. First go and be reconciled to them; then come and offer your gift (Matthew 5:23-24).

We are always to go directly to the one with whom we have an issue. Gossip is not only frowned upon, but forbidden. Gossip enables scapegoating and promotes triangulation, which leads to secondary abuse.

Enabling Abusive Families

Families, unfortunately, are breeding grounds for enabling secondary abuse. It is here, within the family, that most of the unhealthy patterns of interaction are learned. Families with poor boundaries, where people talk about other people behind their backs, are breeding grounds for secondary abuse.

If you were raised in a family where people gossiped about others, criticized others behind their backs, and seemed to have little problem doing so, you know what I mean. You know the vicious power and impact of talking behind a brother's or sister's back. You also know how natural and commonplace such gossip is. What may seem innocuous is anything but that.

Why is gossip and secondary abuse so common in families? Families, like friends and other groups, see what they want to see. If they've been functioning without healthy boundaries, change is not likely to occur. They may, in fact, see little wrong with what they are doing.

Families have patterned ways of interacting, and quite often these patterns are dysfunctional. Consider some of the hurtful ways families interact and enable abuse.

- *Excessive arguing.* Arguing doesn't solve problems. Instead, it creates even more problems. Arguing hurts everyone involved and is very unhealthy. Take a moment to reflect on a situation where an argument erupted and the impact it had on you and your feelings of safety.

- *Excessive criticism.* Criticism, as we know, is an unhealthy way to attempt to facilitate change. Criticism does nothing to bring about effective change; instead, it hurts the person being criticized. Reflect on a time when you were criticized and the impact it had upon your self-esteem.

- *Excessive control.* People need to experience individuality. Families with excessive control restrict autonomy and creativity. When has your individuality been compromised by someone's need for excessive control?
- *Excessive religiosity.* Open expression of faith, including the freedom to express divergent opinions, is healthy. However, religiosity breeds rigidity and conformity. Has anyone ever forced their beliefs on you? How did that affect your personal faith life?

Each of these examples points to ways abuse is enabled. These situations, found in many families, create a lack of safety and are likely to result in someone being emotionally abused. It will be important to be honest with yourself about whether these traits exist in your family. If they do, you need to be honest with yourself and consider changes that must be made.

Your family, like mine, has been functioning in much the same way for years. While we may want them to be different, changing a family is like diverting the Columbia River—it's not likely to happen easily. Be prepared to put in some hard work to create change in a family system.

While change is not easy, we *can* be different within our family. We cannot change others, but we can make healthier choices in our family and notice that when we change, others are likely to change as well. Again, however, we must be honest about what is happening in our family.

It's easy to see what we want to see. Candace Love, in her book *No More Narcissists*, says, "The trap of paying attention to only what we want or how we want things to be will come back to bite us every time."[3]

Love goes on to talk about having healthy boundaries, not only with narcissists and emotionally abusive people but also with those who perpetrate secondary abuse.

> Having healthy boundaries means you have clearly defined your boundaries to yourself and others. When you have healthy boundaries, you don't let people violate them, and

> if they do, you stand up for yourself and firmly tell them you won't tolerate this kind of behavior. Standing up for yourself demonstrates that you respect yourself and that you expect others to respect you as well.[4]

When we maintain healthy boundaries, we will not stand by and allow family or friends to be abused. We will be courageous enough to really see what is taking place and take appropriate action. Secondary abuse ends when we speak out for the victim.

Fickle Friends

Sadly, secondary abuse is not limited to families. It occurs among friends as well. Remember that secondary abuse occurs anytime someone stands by and allows or enables abuse to occur. Failure to intervene in abusive situations is to enable the abuse to occur.

Who has not been betrayed by someone they thought was their friend? Who has not been deeply hurt, perhaps abused, and expected friends to come to their assistance? Most of us, at some time, have had an experience of being betrayed by someone we trusted.

I'm reminded of the biblical story of Job. We find him living a blameless life. He is wealthy, with thousands of sheep, camels, and oxen, and he is considered "the greatest man among all the peoples of the East" (Job 1:3).

Satan enters the scene and taunts God, suggesting Job reveres God only because of how much he is blessed. God accepts the challenge and allows Satan to cause unimaginable destruction to come into Job's life, who subsequently loses all his riches and even his children. Still he continues to bless God.

Job's righteous response seems to confound his friends, who come to him in compassion and sit in silence with him for seven days. Unfortunately, when Job finally opens his mouth, they do too, tormenting him with accusations that he brought his ruin upon himself. Those he had trusted have come to offer help, but they betray him. (Many have had similar experiences with friends whose advice was far less than helpful.)

The story of Job has a happy ending. Job, who gives God the glory for giving and taking away, is richly rewarded for his faithfulness. God gives back to Job twice as much as he had before.

Job was an incredible man and is an inspiration to all of us. Even when he was betrayed by friends and family, even when he suffered from gossipers and those who falsely labeled him a perpetrator of wrongdoing, he continued to bless God. Though crushed by those he trusted, he maintained a steadfast faith. Perhaps you can relate. You've had fickle friends who have hurt you.

Job's story also demonstrates the harmful impact of fickle friends. Job needed people who would comfort him, show compassion, and validate his experience. You need those people too. To do the difficult work discussed in this book, you will need the support of good friends. Supportive friends. Friends who get it.

Lundy Bancroft, in his book *Should I Stay or Should I Go?*, points out this need for support.

> Choose someone who believes in you...You need to share your dreams with someone who is not your partner. There will be important work ahead that will involve your partner, and there will be a time, soon, when you might insist that he show you that he's going to be an active support for your dreams and goals. But for the work we're doing right now, find another friend, one who can focus solely on your dreams.[5]

Bancroft also shares some of the struggles you will face with family and friends—struggles that lead to secondary abuse.

> You may experience that certain relationships with relatives or friends get more difficult as you become increasingly clear about what you need to have happen with your partner. Your choices might not make sense or seem right to them, depending on their own ways of looking at emotional disturbances, abusive attitudes, and addiction. If your partner has had a manipulative style, telling people lies or distorting things about you, you may have the

> additional challenge of having to unravel the messes he has made for you.[6]

Bancroft offers wise counsel when friends or family turn against you. His advice is central to this book.

> When you shift your attention back to your point of view, you are in a stronger position to weather the storms of unfair criticisms that can sometimes follow growth. If you are clearsighted, you will be in a better position to continue to insist on what you need, in spite of the lack of support.[7]

Standing Up Against Secondary Abuse

Intervening against narcissistic and emotional abuse is critical. We must stand up for ourselves and for those who have been abused. We must encourage those who have been abused to cultivate a powerful voice, to speak against those who would dismiss their pain.

Furthermore, we must never participate in gossip and triangulation. We can't allow ourselves to entertain gossip that is hurtful to the innocent victim.

Unfortunately, when it comes to secondary abuse, there are many who don't "get it." They don't understand how tired and weary you feel and how betrayal only adds to your burden. They don't know how hard it is to maintain your voice when others refuse to listen. Somehow, some way, you must stand up against abuse and encourage those few wonderful friends to stand with you.

Standing up against secondary abuse does not mean you can change society. You cannot. It doesn't mean you can change your friends' minds. You can't do that either.

Rather, it means you can choose very carefully who is likely to understand the complexity of narcissism and emotional abuse. You can use discernment when deciding in whom you will confide and to whom you tell your story.

You can also practice being assertive in speaking out against secondary abuse. You can insist that those who scapegoat you face what they have done and set about to make things right. You can insist they stop portraying themselves as innocent victims to friends and family.

All of this work takes keen insight and understanding. You cannot allow yourself to get drawn into the fray. You cannot afford to lose your emotional balance to those with quick and wrongful opinions. Choose carefully who you share your story with and look to for support.

Therapeutic Support

Sadly, family and friends will sometimes let you down. Your church family may also fail to stand up for you when you need them.

It is becoming clearer to me and probably to you that you are primarily responsible for your healing. Others may prove unreliable. Even many professionals, including therapists and pastors, may know less about emotional abuse than you do.

Patricia Evans speaks to this issue in her book *The Verbally Abusive Relationship*. She takes a very strong and appropriate stand.

> In the therapeutic interaction, I do not believe that the therapist should take a neutral position. Nor do I suggest that the therapist take sides with one person against another person. I suggest instead, that the therapist take the side of change...
>
> A person experiencing emotional pain and anguish from encounters with their mate may be able to identify and name what has occurred if they recognize that what has been said to them, or the way they have been treated, is in fact abusive.[8]

Evans understands that secondary abuse can be perpetrated even by well-intentioned therapists. Like pastors, friends, and family, even therapists can be swayed into mislabeling what is occurring right in front of them. They may see a depressed woman as simply depressed, not abused. They may see a couple as needing communication skills when in fact emotional abuse is taking place.

She takes a strong stance when recommending against any therapist (or perhaps friend) who does not see verbal abuse as an act of violence, and against those who hold the partner in any way responsible for the abuser's pervasive pattern of abuse. Finally, she insists the therapist (or friend or family member) must take to heart the partner's experience.[9]

Protecting the Victim

How sad that we have all done what I have done—passing by a wounded woman, failing to step in to offer help. How tragic that we have all listened to the faint stories and refused to put the pieces together and acknowledge what was really taking place.

We don't want to get our hands dirty. We don't want to get our faith dirty. We don't want to risk getting hurt in the process of taking a stand for change.

Here are a few simple steps we can take to stop secondary abuse. Let's agree to use these actions to support victims of narcissistic and emotional abuse.

1. *Validate their experience.* This doesn't take a lot of work. All we have to do is listen carefully and validate what we hear.
2. *Ask some gently probing questions.* Care enough to learn more. Encourage her to tell her story.
3. *Take her experience to heart.* Allow her story to impact you. Don't dismiss it or blame her for anything. Simply allow her to tell her story.
4. *Empathize with her.* If you listen carefully enough, you will understand and be moved by her story. You can empathize with her story because we all have been hurt, betrayed, and wounded at some time in our lives.
5. *Support her.* Ask her how you can help. Get a little dirty in the process.

Protecting the victim, offering support and aid, is not optional. Remember that doing nothing may seem innocent, but it enables the abuse to continue. We cannot stand by and allow victims to suffer.

"Whatever you did for one of the least of these brothers and sisters of mine, you did for me" (Matthew 25:40).

The Path Forward

Narcissistic and emotional abuse is horrible, and it's made much worse when you are alone. Abuse is worsened when those you believed would support you don't. It is made worse by those who refuse to acknowledge it.

We can all make a difference. Let's get our faith and hands a little dirty by refusing to become triangulated, refusing to scapegoat the victim, and choosing to acknowledge abuse when it occurs in our world.

If you are being secondarily abused, have the courage to choose healthy friends who will come alongside you, support you, and protect you. Challenge your friends and family to have courage and take a stand.

Let's now move forward and learn what we can do when even the church is abusive.

8

When the Church Is Abusive

On the day that the intelligence and talents of women are fully honored and employed, the human community and the planet itself will benefit in ways we can only begin to imagine.

ANITA DIAMANT

What image comes to your mind when you think of the word "church"? I will forever picture the enormous brick structure on the corner of Forest and Champion Streets in Bellingham, Washington. Though no longer standing, I will always remember it as a place of peace, inspiration, and refuge.

I can still envision cars pulling up to the corner, dropping off kids and adults. I can see people climbing the steep concrete stairs to the arched entrance and opening the double wooden doors leading to the sanctuary.

I remember the huge sanctuary, rows of pews for the choir, the pastor's study just off to the right, and the large, impressive pulpit he stood behind to deliver the weekly sermons. I can still hear the hymns played on the organ.

I felt God's protective presence in that church. I felt safe. I wanted to be there. Our family went every Sunday morning, Sunday evening, and Wednesday evening. The people of the Bellingham Mission Covenant Church were like a second family to me. I felt loved and cared for, protected and nurtured.

The safety and protection I felt in that church are *not* what many women feel. Many women do not find caring, loving support in their places of worship. For them, the church is abusive, and that is the issue we'll address in this chapter.

Abuse Victims and the Church

Victims of abuse want to feel the protective sanctuary of a church family and pastor. They need a refuge from the harm of their home. Unfortunately, many don't find a safe, listening ear. Many are met with distant, preachy counsel that leaves them feeling unprotected and even more confused.

Victims of narcissistic and emotional abuse need specialized help. They need friends who will come alongside and offer support and guidance. They need family who will understand and offer love—and lots of it. They need their church family to surround them with compassion and spiritual care.

Tragically, the very institution many women look to for support and encouragement, the church, all too often turns its back on the wounded. Too often the church not only fails to protect abused women but also refuses to hold men accountable for their emotional and narcissistic abuse. Often the church offers men protection while shaming women into going back to the abuse, all in the name of faith.

This creates an unfathomable wound to women.

Betrayed in the Church

Jodi and Jake had been an integral part of their church's worship team for years. Jodi's world revolved around her husband, their children, and ministry. She had tolerated his emotionally abusive behavior because she loved their kids, church, and ministry.

Jodi had some of the same feelings toward her church that I had while growing up. She gave much time and energy to their church, sensing a calling to serve there. This was more than a place of worship to her. The people there were a second family to her.

Her ability to tolerate Jake's angry outbursts, emotional eruptions, spending sprees, and erratic behavior came to a screeching halt one

Sunday evening when a friend called, telling her Jake was having an affair with another ministry team member.

This was not the first time rumors had circulated about her husband. This time, however, the rumor seemed tragically real. She feared the worst.

When she first became aware that her husband was spending time alone with one of the other worship team vocalists, she thought speaking to him about it would be enough to cause him to think about how inappropriate it appeared. What she got instead totally knocked her feet out from under her—an admission that he was no longer in love with her and that this other woman was a "better fit."

Jake admitted he wanted a deeper relationship with the other woman. He denied anything physical had taken place, but Jake had been deceptive before with her. He had lied about money and where he spent his time. His deception and troubled behavior had been overwhelming to Jodi, but his attraction to another woman was more than she could tolerate. Jodi was frightened and not sure of her next course of action.

"I never thought I would be the other woman," Jodi told me during our initial counseling session. "We were totally involved in the church, and even though I never felt completely safe with Jake's abusive personality, I did feel safe and protected at church. My friends were there. My faith in the Lord grew so much there."

Jodi paused.

"I never thought about Jake cheating with someone. Then after it came out, I expected the church would step in and support me. I was wrong."

"What happened?" I asked.

"Jake was so matter-of-fact about it when he told me," she said tearfully. "He said his feelings about me had been absent for a long time. My world was crashing down, and he acted like I should be able to take it in stride. I couldn't breathe for days."

She paused to wipe tears from her eyes.

"He made up some nonsense about us being too young when we married," she continued, "about not knowing back then what he really wanted. He said he had been thinking about leaving and seeing if this other woman was a better fit for him.

"I was speechless," she continued. "I didn't see it coming. But his betrayal is just the beginning of my pain."

"What else are you talking about?" I asked, unsure what she was referring to.

"The church meant everything to me," she said. "I loved that church. We gave our time, energy, money, talent...everything to the church. Now they've all turned their back on me. What am I supposed to do?"

Jodi shared that in the beginning, she was completely overwhelmed emotionally and confused about what to do. She wasn't sure what was going on regarding the affair, but she did not wish to slander her husband or the other woman. She didn't want to hurt the music ministry or the church by exposing their crumbling marriage.

"It's all so confusing to me," she continued. "I love my church. I've helped build it. They're family to me. But now they aren't protecting me, and I don't know what to think."

Jodi also felt conflicted about her faith. How could she be angry with God, the pastors, and the church? She was supposed to be under their leadership. What should she do if the leaders weren't protecting her? What was she going to do with all the people she had thought were always available to listen and tend to her? She was terribly confused.

The church leaders were Jake's close friends, which meant they were likely to protect their relationship with him. They seemed reluctant to do anything that might cause him harm and made it clear they were not going to speak out against him. When she talked to them, they seemed to dance around the real issues. She sensed the lines being drawn and found herself on the losing side. She felt alone and afraid.

In the days following, Jodi had time to reflect. She reviewed all the years she had felt abandoned by her husband, a man who enjoyed the limelight of being onstage at home, at work, and in the church. She recalled many times when Jake left her alone while he worked long hours at his job and then at the church.

Jodi recalled his constant irritability and frequent angry outbursts. When confronting him, she risked facing his defensiveness and accusations. If she dared to confront him, he accused her of being an unsupportive, biblically unsubmissive wife. She knew she hadn't been a priority to Jake, but now she felt totally alone.

Betrayed by the Church

Often, a woman's church is one of the few places she can go for help when she realizes something is very wrong in her marriage. Her hope is that the leadership will provide the context for healing, surrounding her family with correction, support, accountability, and love by shepherding them to health and godliness.

"I thought I could go to the pastor for help," Jodi said. "We are taught to bring problems to the leadership of the church. But I've been very disappointed. I'd gone to the pastor before for help about Jake's controlling behavior, and I was passed off to the associate pastor. He didn't offer much advice."

"What kind of counsel did you get?" I asked.

She shook her head.

"The associate pastor couldn't believe Jake could be that controlling, and he encouraged me to pray for a change. He didn't want to hear about any specifics. He left me with some Scriptures and said he'd pray for me."

"I'm sorry," I said. "I've heard many stories like that. Many pastors aren't trained in emotional abuse and don't know how to help."

"But they didn't do anything about Jake's affair either," she said with exasperation. "I couldn't believe it. They promised me they would handle the situation. I waited for weeks for them to confront him and tell him he had to change. But they didn't do anything. They didn't discipline him. They didn't even monitor him to make sure he stopped the affair."

Jodi's response from her church is tragically common. Desperately seeking help, women like Jodi often find instead an unwillingness by the church to get too involved. Many women are patronized and told everything will be okay. They find church leadership refusing to delve deeply into matters or take critical stands.

Jodi's interactions with church leadership left her feeling deeply hurt and abandoned. She sensed their loyalty to her husband and their neglect of her. She sensed the leadership was reluctant to take a position that might harm their ministry.

Jodi felt torn in sharing her feelings with me. She wanted to believe the best of her church but couldn't shake the feeling that her church leaders were reluctant to get involved with troubled marriages.

Support for the Perpetrator

Jodi's problems seemed to only get worse. Already wounded from years of abuse and control by her husband, she struggled now with his blatant rejection and betrayal. Add to this her feeling alone and betrayed by her church. The church's support for her husband made her wounds far worse.

Where were the leaders she expected to protect her and help her save her marriage? Even though her ministers initially seemed supportive and showed outrage at his behavior, she noticed little change and no real intervention.

It was this *apparent* support, combined with the leader's supportive language, that caused her to expect so much more from them. She was prepared for supportive action, but none was forthcoming.

This led to another layer of abuse.

"I really expected the pastors to ask Jake to step out of ministry," she said. "That's what I thought was standard practice. How can they support a man leading worship who is having an affair with someone else on the worship team? The staff was more concerned with how things appeared than they were with Jake's infidelity. The staff didn't want to cause any kind of riff in the church. They never explained their actions to me. Now I don't trust their leadership."

Paul Hegstrom comments on situations like this in his book *Angry Men and the Women Who Love Them: Breaking the Cycle of Physical and Emotional Abuse.*

> It is a sad state of affairs in the church when a woman has been abused, it seems that the congregation, her friends, and the clergy shy away from dealing with the situation.

> She feels forsaken by those she should be able to lean on the most.[1]

Jodi expected to be protected by her church family from her husband's emotional abuse. She expected friends and church family to circle around her and help her emotionally and spiritually. She hoped church friends she had helped over the years would now rush in to help her. That didn't happen.

Jodi also expected her church leadership to firmly step in and discipline her husband and then supervise his restoration. She expected them to encourage counseling for him and then for them as a couple. She thought they would firmly and decisively take immediate action. She discovered that her issues were apparently less important than other church matters.

Jodi is baffled and perplexed, feeling betrayed and deeply hurt. While she expected understanding, compassion, support, and confrontation of her husband's affair, little was forthcoming. Perhaps her deepest betrayal came, however, when the church supported her husband because of his "difficult, unsubmissive wife" and protected or denied his abusive behavior rather than speaking out against it. He was allowed to remain on the worship team, and his affair was pushed underground.

Tragically, Jodi had to navigate her husband's affair alone. She separated from him in an effort to maintain her sanity, feeling very little support from her longtime friends at church and none from the church leadership. All this created another layer of emotional abuse.

False Friends, False Hope

We expect our friends, especially longtime friends, to provide support. We depend on them for our emotional and spiritual strength when we are low.

When I think about my friends, I consider those I know I can turn to in times of need. I trust them. I know they will do what they say they will do, be who they say they will be, and perform the actions they say they will perform.

What happens if those we believe will be there for us disappear in times of trouble? What happens if those people have promised to do something for us, only to fade away when there is a significant need?

This creates incredible tension in our minds and can exacerbate emotional trauma. We depend on truth to survive in this world. We depend upon people telling us the truth, doing what they say they will do, and being where they say they will be. We depend on them looking out for our best interests and welfare.

This kind of truth is essential to our mental and spiritual health.

Something tragic happens when truth is replaced with a lie, facts replaced with distortion, and our best interests replaced with someone's hidden agenda.

I remember clearly some years back when my office manager, who I counted on to be trustworthy, reliable, and protective of me, was discovered to be embezzling from my company. This was a woman who had shared the inner workings of my business and had helped me grow the company.

As I uncovered dishonorable fact after fact, my heart sank. I was flooded with emotions of disbelief, anger, discouragement, and profound betrayal.

"How could this be?" I said to my wife. "I trusted her. I counted on her to do what she said she was doing. She told me she was fiercely protective of me and my company. She said she would always look after my best interests. She said she championed me and our work in the community."

She lied.

This story, while true and traumatic for me, cannot compare to the woman who married and believed her mate would protect and love her in all circumstances. My story is nothing compared to the countless stories I've heard and witnessed from victims of narcissistic and emotional abuse.

Jodi shared the following story about her friends.

"When my friends heard Jake and I separated, some called immediately, offering hope. They seemed genuinely concerned about me, and I thought they were calling to find out how I was doing. But they were really calling to preach at me and tell me what to do. They sent Scriptures, not necessarily to encourage me but to influence me and bring me back to the fold. They really only wanted to push their message—that I should follow the leadership and do whatever they said I should do."

"This sounds very frightening," I said.

"I don't think I feel frightened," she continued, "but I do feel hurt and confused. Am I supposed to listen to them? They don't take the time to listen to me or empathize with my situation. They say they offer hope and caring, but I don't feel it. I don't think they can see what they are doing. I don't trust them."

"I am really sorry, Jodi," I said. "Your story is one I've heard so many times—people in the church believing they are doing what is right, when it is so hurtful. The church needs a lot of education on emotional abuse."

"It's a show," she said angrily. "They say what they are doing is for the purposes of God, but that's not really what it is. They believe they are being holy and spiritual, but I don't feel heard. I don't feel understood. They don't want to hear anything that goes against how they view the church and church leadership."

Jodi's words were piercing to me. I have been part of church leadership. I have been an ambassador for the church. Have I been part of an abusive culture without knowing it? I let her words sink in. Her message was strong and clear and extremely disconcerting.

Patriarchy and the Church

Jodi was angry at the church—me, you, and others who form the church. She was deeply troubled at the lack of help that she received from the shepherds of the flock.

She is certainly not the first who has been deeply disappointed with the church. Are her expectations too high, or did her church let her down? If her church failed her, are they also guilty of participating in her abuse?

I realize these are tough questions and perhaps unsettling. Her words certainly caused me to stop and think. While challenged, I also felt defensive of the church. The church is fallible, and Jodi cannot expect it to be perfect. That will never happen. How much can we expect the church to do in situations of emotional abuse?

I sat and listened as Jodi shared her feelings and thoughts, sifting them through my well-established belief system. Nothing she said fit my viewpoint, but she was intense and incisive and had taken the time to consider her position.

"Our church is led by men, and Jake is part of the club," she said. "I don't feel heard. My voice has effectively been silenced, and I don't trust them now to care for me. Where are those who were supposed to love and protect me?"

Her thoughts and question were clear and firm and terribly unsettling. I had to reconsider what was happening to Jodi and what perhaps has happened to you.

Is it significant that Jake is a man, that his church is led by men, and that it's part of a larger culture dominated by men?

Does it mean anything that he is in leadership?

Sadly, the answer to each of these questions is unequivocally yes. While I have critical things to say about the church, I want to assure you that I love the church. We are all the church. But the church is flawed in many ways, just as we are.

The church has a history of treating men and women differently. Men are often given preferential treatment. Patriarchy endorses men running the church, holding positions of authority and leadership, and maintaining a masculine feel to the church. Women are often reduced, marginalized, and subordinated to men.

Rachel Held Evans, in her article "Patriarchy and Abusive Churches," speaks to this pointedly.

> Christian patriarchy is often illustrated as a series of umbrellas in which the male leadership of the church holds authority over the male leaders of the homes who hold authority of the women and children at the bottom of the hierarchy.
>
> This authority structure is typically described as a series of "coverings" or "protections" but unfortunately, the effect

> is often the opposite, as abused women and children find they have no recourse or power, as every decision in their lives must be made by a series of men, many of whom are more invested in protecting the reputation of the ministry than the people in it.[2]

Does this describe what might be happening to Jodi? I think so. Does it tragically describe many women in one form of abuse or another? Again, yes.

Patriarchy often stems from an incorrect interpretation of Scripture. Hegstrom again weighs in on this topic.

> Many times in a church world, submission is held over the heads of women by men who are emotionally manipulative or abusive in order to get their way and maintain power and control. Ephesians 5:24-28 reminds us that as Christ died for the Church, a man should give his life for his wife.[3]

I am a man and have been steeped in patriarchal church history. I was raised in a patriarchal church, attended a patriarchal Bible school, and studied at a patriarchal seminary. I've only heard two women preach sermons in my 60-plus years of life. I'm afraid I have patriarchy running through my veins and don't even know it. Is it time to critically review how we do church?

Reconsidering Your Spirituality

Perhaps by now I've stepped on your spiritual toes, or perhaps you've resonated with Jodi's story and are glad it is finally being told. Either way, I encourage you to question and reconsider your spirituality. Maybe what we've always thought to be true is not. Maybe the way we conduct church needs to be reconsidered.

This is a challenge for many, including me. Like me, you may cling to certain spiritual doctrines: men are to lead the church, spiritual leadership is to be obeyed, spiritual leaders know more because they have been trained and have a direct line to God, resistance to spiritual leadership is tantamount to sin.

This can be heavy stuff. Who wants to be seen as a rebel?

When it comes to the topic of emotional abuse in the church, however, it is past time for us all to review our beliefs. It is beyond time for us to listen very, very carefully to those who are being abused. Not only to those who have been abused in the past, but also to those sitting next to us in the pews who are being abused even now.

It is all too common for those in a Christian environment to send an abused wife the message that being godly looks like enduring more, praying more, and letting God step in. Many give her the message that she must "stay and pray," tolerating whatever happens in her home. Some believe that what happens behind the closed doors of the home is a private and personal matter, not to be tampered with. Many believe that God alone is the one to convict the man of abusive behavior, that it is not her job to speak out against his abusive behavior.

Will van der Hart makes this assertion in his article "Words Matter—Emotional Abuse and the Church."

> Accusations of emotional abuse in churches are rarely taken seriously because of a common myth that "church leaders are always the victims of malign accusations" or that this is simply "spiritual attack." It is very rarely accepted that church leaders are emotionally broken individuals who often cause significant damage to others through their words and actions.[4]

Clearly we all have a responsibility to work for an emotionally healthy culture both within ourselves and within our churches, being fully aware of what makes for emotionally abusive conduct. We must serve everyone in the church, and that includes both perpetrators and victims of abuse.

The church is spiritually blind and emotionally abusive when it perpetuates the idea that being a godly, submissive woman means taking whatever abuse a husband has yet to be convicted about. It is sinful to protect the church from getting into the fray by minimizing the harm or giving religious platitudes about God's power. Yes, abusive marriages are messy and brutal. But that is exactly what God calls His church to stand against.

Seeing the Church Differently

Questioning your spirituality means seeing the church differently. The church is not for perfect people. It's for the broken, hurting, lost, and sinful to be set free to live as God designed and called them to. The leadership has a responsibility to shepherd the people—to protect them from sin and abuse, to bring shelter and healing for the broken and hurting, and to care for the matters of the heart. It is never their calling to affirm or enable sin of any kind! Not religiosity, self-righteous facades, or outright abuse.

For the church to point fingers at women in distress is to completely ignore the damage to the most powerful representation of God to the world—the Christian marriage. Typically, churches put an immense amount of weight on marriage in terms of physical ties. They put very little emphasis on the emotional ties, or that marriage is meant to be about exemplifying God's love to the world. They might preach love from the pulpit, but where the rubber meets the road, they gloss over destructiveness and abuse within marriage as if God is okay with it as long as they stay together.

But how does that marriage look to God? God cares more about the individuals involved, their relationship, and how it represents Him than He does a piece of paper signed by a judge. And if you are persistent about a wife being submissive, you must be even more persistent about starting from the top down, pointing your finger at the husband's abuse for what it really is. The divorce God hates is the divorce of the relationship.

Entering the Sanctuary

I love the word "sanctuary"—for me a sanctuary is a place of peace, safety, and protection. It provides an opportunity to sit with God. Not that God sits only in His sanctuary, but throughout history the sanctuary has been the special place reserved for those seeking God.

Abused women desperately need a place of peace, safety, and protection. They need an opportunity to sit with *Abba*, their heavenly Father. Consider that in the midst of their narcissistic and emotional abuse, they have experienced very little peace, safety, and protection.

To enter the sanctuary, however, there must *be* a sanctuary. There must be a place, physically, spiritually, and emotionally, where women are protected and feel safe.

I have some ideas about what that sanctuary might look like, what church leadership might do to create a safe place for abused women to feel loved, supported, and deeply cared for.

Pastors can help men better understand their biblical role in marriage by providing balanced teaching on Ephesians 5:22-28, offering marriage classes and counseling, and modeling a loving relationship with their wives. Additionally, here are a few practical tools churches can use to help narcissistic and emotional abuse victims and to hold perpetrators accountable for change.

- *Validate her feelings.* I find it extremely rare for victims of abuse to exaggerate or lie about their experiences.
- *Take a keen interest in the victim's story.* Take the time to listen to what she has to say. Her story will unfold and make sense as you listen with care.
- *Determine the danger of her situation.* Is this woman safe? Does immediate intervention need to occur? What is the next step to be taken?
- *Learn all you can about the topic of narcissistic and emotional abuse.* Create an atmosphere where women can speak out about their experiences.
- *Include a study on family violence and the prevention of violence in the adult Sunday school curriculum.* Make topics of emotional abuse in marriage part of the group studies within the church.
- *Offer support and unconditional love.* Connect victims with

support groups and prayer partners, and provide ongoing emotional and practical support. Prepare to offer ongoing support through the process of healing, in addition to helping the victim to find professional counseling.

- *Hold the abuser accountable, utilizing principles based on Matthew 18:15-17.* Remove the individual from leadership as appropriate. However, the ultimate goal of confrontation, as emphasized in Galatians 6:1, is repentance and restoration.
- *Men must enter into specific treatment for emotional abuse.* Church leadership must hold these men accountable for change.
- *Make an appropriate referral to a Christian counselor, highly trained in emotional abuse.* Both the perpetrator and victim will need ongoing professional help and support, and the church can be part of this process.

Churches must develop a protocol, utilizing these tools, for working with abused women and abusive men. They can no longer ignore the severity and magnitude of this issue.

Men, women, and children caught in the cycle of emotional abuse need practical, emotional, and spiritual support. Victims want and need support from their churches. Take steps to make your church a safe place, where victims and their abusers can find grace, love, and healing.

The Path Forward

I have undoubtedly stepped on your toes a few times. I, along with women like Jodi, have dared to challenge spiritual leadership that is misguided, misinformed, and mistaken.

We know, however, that change cannot take place until we all recognize something is dreadfully wrong. I'm rethinking my spirituality and hoping you will do the same. If you are one of the brave women willing to speak out, please continue. If you are not yet ready to speak out, know there is a movement afoot to create a healthier church for you.

Join me now as we talk about another impact of narcissistic and emotional abuse—growing smaller and smaller.

9

Growing Smaller and Smaller

The Spirit God gave us does not make us timid, but gives us power, love and self-discipline.

2 TIMOTHY 1:7

Sherri got married the summer before her senior year of college.

"Everyone would have told you my husband and I were a perfect match," she told me. "We just clicked, had lots of fun together, and were headed the same direction in life. I believed Joe was my biggest fan."

A few months after graduating from college, having been married just over a year, Sherri acknowledged the flaw in their relationship. Her hopes of going to grad school were quickly dismissed, her desire to have children was put off until he said it was time, and everything about her life was shifted to fit his plan.

"As long as my dreams and hopes matched Joe's idea of how life should go, we were great. But as soon as I mentioned anything that went against his plans, I was told it was ridiculous, wouldn't work, wasn't good...whatever he could say to dissuade me."

It wasn't just her goals in life that were devalued, but also her opinions and way of thinking, her family and friends, the way she kept house and managed money, and even acts of intimacy.

"He corrected everything I said and did, like he held the rule book and I didn't have a clue. His way of living was right, and mine was wrong."

At first she went along with it.

"I thought it was the right thing to do. I thought it was biblical submission. I wanted my life to revolve around his. That's how I was raised."

Now years later, facing a divorce, she realizes, "I don't know who I am anymore. I can barely remember what my hopes and dreams were. I'm isolated from my friends, my family, and my church. I spent my entire marriage trying to make him happy, and now I feel worthless."

She paused.

"Look at me," she said tearfully. "He's gone, doing fine, and I'm struggling to figure out my life. I'm pathetic."

Erosion of a Life

Of course, Sherri is not pathetic. However, she is lost. She feels small and insignificant, and that is what this chapter is about. It's about how one loses her life and how to find it again.

How did Sherri lose her life? How could she forget what she wanted to do and be? What happened to her dreams?

Napoleon Hill is reported to have said, "The starting point of all achievement is desire." But what if that desire has evaporated, one drop at a time? What if there is no one to champion your dreams, no cheerleader to encourage you?

Sadly, passion fades. If we don't nurture our dreams, leaving them unfulfilled and unnourished, our dreams will fade. If we aren't active in pursuing our dreams, they will diminish.

Sherri shared more with me.

"I wanted to go to grad school and become a social worker or early education teacher. I've always wanted to protect and help vulnerable children. I don't know what it is about kids who have had a hard time, but I wanted to help them somehow. Maybe I would have been a special education teacher. But Joe's career always took precedence. He said maybe sometime down the road I could go back to school. It was always, 'Not now.'"

"Did you push to go back to school?" I asked.

"Not really," she said. "Joe made it clear that his career came first. There was never any question about that, and the church supported him. 'Support your man.' I was swimming upstream just thinking about grad school or considering a career."

"So, what happened to your dreams?" I asked.

"I told myself they weren't that important," she said. "Being a good wife and mother was enough. Now I have the nagging thought that I've missed out on life."

And by Comparison

How did Sherri know she was not where she wanted to be? What gave her the impression that she had somehow lost out on life?

"I looked around at some of my friends who *did* go to grad school," she said. "They have families and at least part-time careers. I'm envious of them. I did exactly what Joe wanted me to do. I gave in to his pressure to stay home and raise our girls."

Sherri peered off into space and continued to reflect on her life.

"I don't know what happened to my life," she said wistfully. "I wonder what I could have done if I hadn't given in to his every demand. Compared to my friends, I sometimes feel like I've wasted my life."

Of course, Sherri had not wasted her life, though she had made concession after concession to Joe and had missed out on some important opportunities. She lived in Joe's shadow. She lived the life he expected her to live. She grew smaller and smaller while he grew larger.

"I raised my children right," she said proudly. "I can't say everything was lost. My kids are happy and on their own. They love me but don't rely on me as they did years ago. I'm living in an empty nest, and that only adds to my sadness."

While Sherri appeared primarily sad, I wondered about feelings of anger and resentment.

"Do you feel any anger or resentment?" I asked.

"Oh yeah," she replied quickly. "I can't believe I'm sitting here at 40 years old and divorced. He's a successful banker, making great money with a great future. I'm a stay-at-home mom with no one left at home. I have no job, no resume, and no experience."

Sherri's story is a familiar one to me. She capitulated to her husband's domination and must now pick up the pieces of her life and start again.

The Dominant Narcissist

According to Sherri, Joe seems to have no regrets. He now wants to live alone. She wonders what is really going through his mind. He lived his life as if his way was the only one that mattered.

"What did it feel like to be married to him?" I asked Sherri.

"Dominated," she replied quickly. "He was selfish and self-centered. It was always his way. Anytime I brought up a concern, his reaction was bigger than my concern. His emotions were bigger than mine. His beliefs were bigger than mine. His arguments were more powerful and persuasive than mine. He sucked the air out of the room and the life out of me."

Sherri discovered she couldn't influence him, so she quit trying. She had to keep Joe happy if she wanted any peace in her home. She had hoped he might listen to her if she gave in enough, but no amount of giving up of herself influenced him.

Sherri made a goal to love Joe fully, giving in to him emotionally and physically. Again, loving and submitting to him did not move him to compassion toward her. He would fuss and brood anytime he didn't get exactly what he wanted. During those times, he was sarcastic and hurtful. She wondered if he saw everything about her as a constant threat to his own sense of self.

Joe seems to have been something like the biblical character Nabal. Both men illustrate how foolish narcissism can make a man. In 1 Samuel 25, we read a brief story about Nabal and his wife, Abigail.

Nabal is described as "the man churlish and evil in his doings" (1 Samuel 25:3 ASV). "Churlish," by the way, means a bear of a man—harsh, rude, and brutal—and his record proves he was all of that. He was stubborn, ill-tempered, surly, and mean in his dealings with others.

In contrast, his wife was almost exactly the opposite. She was an intelligent and beautiful woman. You can imagine the eggshells she had to walk on around him!

Like many narcissists, Nabal was rich with goods and gold, thinking only of his possessions. He was also a drunk and an unbeliever, and he was jealous of King David's success. Nabal refused to show respect to King David and his men. He asserted his dominance with a foolishness that would bring destruction upon his whole home.

Yet despite her husband's lack of judgment and maturity, Abigail was loyal to him. As a Hebrew woman whose culture restricted her from offering counsel, she risked the wrath of her narcissistic husband and the king by pleading for her husband's life. She showed incredible courage in the face of danger.

Somehow, I presume through God's sovereign hand, she remained strong even in the shadow of Nabal's selfishness. In the end, Nabal was destroyed, and Abigail married King David.

Sounds like a great love story. Her life undoubtedly improved, marrying Israel's most illustrious king. She married David in faith, and God certainly ordained it.

The Power of Inferiority

Sherri and perhaps even Abigail struggled with feelings of inferiority. Living with a powerful and dominant man will weaken anyone's esteem.

Many talk about feelings of inferiority in a superficial way, as if we could will them away by positive thinking. Feelings of inferiority can drain the zest and vigor from you. Inferiority is damaging to the psyche, draining away positive self-regard.

"You can do it," we may say to a friend lacking self-confidence. "You're as good as anybody else and need to act that way. Fake it until you make it."

We hope our words will encourage them, shaking them from feelings of inferiority to feelings of worth. But feelings of inferiority are really a serious matter, especially if these feelings are protracted and entrenched, as appeared to be the case with Sherri.

Remember that Sherri graduated from college—no small feat. She had enough self-esteem and determination to plan for a career. What happened? How did she lose her self-confidence? Joe stole her self-confidence one ounce at a time.

Sherri's self-esteem didn't disappear all at once but rather was eroded over time. Her physical energy was depleted little by little. Her ability to bounce back was challenged again and again. By the time she came to see me, she had nearly lost her will to live. This is not unusual for women suffering under the prolonged stress of emotional abuse.

Feelings of inferiority are rooted in an experience of weakness, helplessness, and dependency. Let's take a closer look at each of these feelings.

- *Weakness.* It is easy to see how Sherri and other women might struggle with this issue. Women experience extreme emotional fatigue as well as physical fatigue. Their bodies begin to deteriorate with the emotional trauma. Prolonged illness is debilitating. Fighting against abusive men is emotionally and physically draining, leaving them vulnerable to even greater illnesses. Emotionally abusive men often prey on and promote weakness in women.

- *Helplessness.* Emotional and physical fatigue naturally creates feelings of helplessness. Women want to rise above their problems but gradually feel beaten down and helpless. Feelings of helplessness naturally create feelings of depression. Depression often creates debilitating anxiety and insecurity. The more fatigued you feel, the more helpless you feel, and your choices seem to diminish.

- *Dependency.* Victims of narcissistic and emotional abuse often develop an unhealthy dependency upon the abusive man. Abusive men often cultivate this dependency, knowing it is likely to help them maintain control. Victims of abuse lose their creative energy to see viable options for change.

Martha Brockenbrough, in her article "Is Your Partner Emotionally Abusive?," notes that typical effects of emotional abuse are devastating and include symptoms of depression, anxiety, and destroyed self-esteem.

> Over time, this tiptoeing around can devastate a woman, making her anxious, fatigued, and depressed...Women who are being emotionally abused often feel trapped, and they change how they behave, speak, dress, socialize, and even work in an effort to dodge the hurtful language and behavior. As a result, they gradually lose their identities."[1]

Can you see how a woman can lose her sense of self and her feelings of self-confidence, leading to feelings of inferiority?

Cognitive Dissonance

Feelings of inferiority are one aspect of the gradual erosion of self. Another devastating aspect of the loss of self is *cognitive dissonance*—feelings of unreality, confusion, and a mindset of not trusting your own perception.

Cognitive dissonance is tantamount to feeling as if you were going crazy. When suffering from cognitive dissonance, you no longer are confident of having a grasp on reality. You feel differing and conflicting emotions, think differing and conflicting thoughts, and struggle to reconcile them. The impact is horrific.

What causes cognitive dissonance?

The abuser is forever telling you that what you think is wrong, what you see is not true, and what you believe is not based in reality. Think about it—being told again and again that you cannot trust your own perceptions will seriously impact your sense of self and feelings of worth. Being constantly questioned and harangued will devastate your self-confidence and ability to evaluate your world.

Cognitive dissonance can be further defined as holding two or more contradictory thoughts or beliefs at one time, as Andrea Schneider points out in her article "Unreality Check: Cognitive Dissonance in Narcissistic Abuse": "The result is a state of anxious confusion and a desire to reduce the resultant overwhelm and unbalanced perception."[2]

Tina is a 30-year-old woman with two young children, the victim of narcissistic and emotional abuse. When she and her husband, Nick, met, he swept her off her feet with his charm. After a brief and fiery courtship, filled with intense passion as well as intense conflict, he pushed for marriage. She succumbed, believing their conflicts would subside after getting married.

She was wrong. His charm subsided, but his temper did not. Much of the good he brought to their early relationship evaporated, but his nastiness remained. Still, she loved him. They built a home together and had two children. They shared many good and bad experiences. Though much of her world was intertwined with his, it wasn't enough to make her stay.

"I left Nick a few weeks ago," she told me. "I still love him but just can't live with him because of his constant criticism and possessiveness. It seems like that would be enough for me to let go of him," she said. "But I can't stop thinking about him and wishing he would change. I love him and hate him at the same time. It's driving me crazy."

Tina is experiencing cognitive dissonance. She is holding contradictory perceptions—love and hate, attraction and repulsion—in her mind at the same time. Wanting to be close to him while wanting to run for the hills. She wants to call him but hopes he will leave her alone. The result of these opposing feelings creates a great deal of anxiety for her and others caught in the web of emotional abuse.

Schneider goes on to share more about this state of anxiety for the victim of abuse.

> The partner is courted, romanced, and ultimately falls in love with the abuser, not knowing that the abuser has ulterior motives. The partner envisions wedding details and enjoys the courtship, flowers, and being placed on a pedestal. The abuser then suddenly makes a comment denying that he or she said anything about getting married. He or she goes on to say that the partner is "crazy" for thinking that. Blame is then projected upon the partner, and the partner is dizzy with confusion.[3]

The result is cognitive dissonance. This emotional abuse renders the woman confused and reeling with headache and heartache.

Perhaps the above example is extreme, yet I assure you such events happen. If it did not happen to you on such a grand scale, it may have happened to you in a simpler yet pervasive manner. Your mate may tell you something did not happen that did, or something was said that was not said, all leading to a hazy view of reality and debilitating confusion.

Cognitive dissonance is exhausting and debilitating and makes you feel crazy.

Crazy Making

The process of growing smaller and smaller is further exacerbated by *crazy making*—emotional abuse that distorts the truth and leads you to question yourself. It often puts you in a no-win situation.

People make jokes about crazy makers, bringing up examples about Crazy Uncle Larry or Eccentric Aunt Marge. While people may quip about crazy makers, there is nothing humorous about it. Quite the opposite—crazy making makes people feel crazy.

In my book *Dealing with the CrazyMakers in Your Life*, I cite five kinds of crazy makers:

1. *The aggressor.* The aggressor is the bully who pushes his way past you with sheer force, demanding emotional and sometimes physical space. He overwhelms you, dominates you, and takes up every bit of space in any situation. You have no emotional room and no place of importance. You must become smaller.

2. *The egotist.* The egotist is large in his thinking and presentation, grasping at emotional space and attention. He has the best ideas, the greatest thoughts, a corner on all knowledge. You must become smaller.

3. *The sufferer.* The sufferer also takes up all the emotional space but does so by the force of his problems. His problems are bigger than yours, they are unsolvable, and they demand attention. He will whine, pout, and complain to get attention. You must become smaller.

4. *The borderline.* The borderline is erratic and unpredictable,

demanding emotional space by his crazy behavior. You never know what will set him off. When he is explosive, you will not know how to calm him down. His erratic nature leaves little room for you. You must become smaller.

5. *The control freak.* The control freak demands emotional space by his need and insistence that things go his way. He has mastered the art of persuasion. He has airtight arguments and is willing to use them to control you. You must become smaller.

Kellie Jo Holly describes crazy making in her insightful blog post "CrazyMaking: Domestic Abuse Intended to Cause Self-Doubt."

> Crazymaking throws you off balance mentally or emotionally making you easier to control...If you're a victim of crazymaking, you often feel lost, disconnected, unsure of your standing in the relationship and of yourself...Crazymaking makes you feel like you are the crazy one.[4]

Think back to the story of Tina. Crazy making occurred when her mate told her what he wanted, she did it, and it still wasn't enough. Crazy makers are rarely satisfied. They have emotional needs that cannot be filled regardless of how hard you try. You will always do something wrong and feel their disapproval.

What you do is never the way they want it. They question why it took you so long to do it, or they will find something else to complain about. This is beyond maddening, and your response, if less than perfect, will add another complex layer to the chaos.

When dealing with a crazy maker—a narcissistic and emotional abuser—you constantly feel disoriented. Nothing is predictable or stable. Try as you might, you will not be able to figure out the code to his happiness. You cannot do enough, give enough, or tiptoe light enough to satisfy him. Interactions are not understandable, predictable, or normal. He has one set of rules for himself and another for you.

The bottom line is, crazy making makes you feel crazy!

Energy Vampires

Crazy makers have also been called *energy vampires*, sucking the life and energy out of us. There are people in our lives who give energy and people who take it. Crazy makers—narcissistic and emotional abusers—steal energy from us.

Crazy making, coupled with criticism, packs an overwhelming punch. You know what I mean—you can be happy about something, and they find a way to douse your enthusiasm with cold water. When you are excited about a new idea, these energy vampires go on to tell you all the things wrong with your idea, sucking the life out of you and your dreams.

Just as a child's heart will wither with ongoing criticism, adult hearts are broken when faced with a critical attitude. When children's fragile ideas are stomped on, they will retreat. When they tell you they want to become president of the United States someday and you tell them they are being silly, you destroy their imagination and dreams. It is the same with an adult.

What is going on in the heart of these critical, energy-draining people?

Typically, these energy vampires take away your energy and excitement because they are emotionally stingy. Perhaps they are unhappy, resentful, or jealous of what is happening to you.

Rather than listen to his spouse's heart, the emotional abuser tends to filter his world as a constant threat to his sense of self. When the victim takes the chance to be vulnerable, sharing what she thinks or living life without fear or hiding, the perpetrator reacts with contempt and criticism.

Sadly, the critical, emotionally abusive mate lives in a world of emotional stinginess. He withholds praise and dishes out criticism. As a result of his hurtful behavior, you grow smaller and smaller, diminished and shrinking.

More on Growing Smaller

Growing smaller doesn't happen all at once, just as a child doesn't lose self-esteem because of just one incident. Abuse is a process, and so is the loss of one's self.

Growing smaller happens like the erosion of a rock when water continuously spills over it. The edges that gave the rock its definition slowly erode. The beautiful colors of the rock fade into gray.

Perhaps it has been like that for you. The color, definition, shape, and edges that created you have been worn away. You have tried and tried to stop his aggression, his egotism, his unhappiness, his erratic behavior, and even his control, but the result has been you losing yourself.

Brain Fog

There is another reason many victims lose themselves, watching their life grow smaller and smaller. As if the loss of self is not enough, as well as loss of self-esteem and confidence, these problems often lead to something even more debilitating—*brain fog*, or feelings of confusion, forgetfulness, and lack of focus.

Consider that our bodies, including our brains, have been wonderfully created. They have been created to function in optimal conditions, but not conditions of ongoing, high-alert stress. As you experience prolonged emotional abuse, your body is pumping out adrenaline and cortisol. You feel increasingly anxious, weary, and overwhelmed. It is no wonder your brain screams out, "Enough!"

Many women have told me that under these circumstances they simply run out of emotional energy. They can no longer carry on as they did prior to the abuse. Once they were excited about life, but now, simply coping is a daily challenge.

"Brain fog is an inability to really punch through," says Mady Hornig, associate professor of epidemiology at Columbia University Medical Center in New York City. "It's a vague sense of what you're trying to retrieve, but you can't focus in on it, and the effort to harness the thought can be as draining as physical activity."[5]

Sadly, brain fog is a perfectly natural response to narcissistic and emotional abuse. It is your brain's way of saying to the foreign intruder (the abuser), "Get out of my head!" Your brain is responding naturally to someone telling you that what you're feeling, thinking, and doing is totally wrong.

Brain fog from narcissistic and emotional abuse is not something you can simply snap out of, because your brain is trying to protect you from further trauma. You have become numb. Shutting down is an involuntary way to protect yourself, almost like a piece of machinery shutting itself off before it overheats. Your brain is responding naturally to danger and threat.

Loss of Self

Brain fog and growing smaller are terrifying experiences. Consider how important it is to be able to think clearly, make important, critical decisions, and map out your life. Imagine being unable to think clearly enough to carry on your job, to manage your home and your children.

One woman shared this story with me.

"I feel like I lost myself. I looked in the mirror and didn't recognize myself. I used to be funny, witty, and kind. Now I feel serious, somber, and irritable. Who is this person? What happened to me?"

She paused before sharing further.

"I'm happy when my boyfriend treats me nice. I start to get a glimpse of my old self. When he is friendly and kind, I'm on top of the world. But then he gets mad over nothing, and I sink back down. I hate that my moods and very self are that dependent on him."

This dependency is natural. After all, we were created by God to be in relationship. We were not created, however, to be abused. We were not created not to know from one day to the next whether we would be treated well.

In this fight for your life, it is nearly impossible to pursue your dreams. In this struggle for your self, it is impossible to focus on what you want to do with your life, let alone do it. But you must dig deep into your creative reservoir, which is still there, to find those parts of you that are desperate to come alive again.

You cannot give up on yourself. You must fight on. Despite brain fog, weakness, fatigue, and emotional struggle, you must push forward.

Recapturing Your Life

Thankfully, there are many things you can do to recapture and rebuild your life. Try practicing each of these strategies every day.

- *Don't take things personally.* It is tempting, having a soft heart, to take his messages personally. It's hard not to. Remember that his behavior is about him, not you.
- *Stay clear.* His critical messages may confuse you. When you confront him, he can be like Teflon, rebuffing anything you say. He defends himself against your efforts to stop his critical messages, and as a result, you often become confused. Remind yourself of what you know and believe, remaining clear and strong.
- *Believe your truth.* Hearing the distorted, convoluted message again and again, you begin to believe him. You may be tempted to believe he's right. His words begin to settle into you, leading to confusion and loss of self-confidence. Don't do it. Hold on to your truth.
- *Set boundaries.* Because of his overwhelming power, it's hard to set boundaries. He plows through the boundaries you attempt to erect, making you even more vulnerable. Learn to build taller, stronger, firmer boundaries. Each time you do, your boundary-building muscles grow.
- *Leave their presence.* Because of your growing weakness, fatigue, and discouragement, you stay with him. You become worn down, depleted, and small. Don't succumb to him. Choose when, where, and how you will be with him.

These are just a few of the ways you can regain and maintain power in your life.

Remember You Before the Abuse

Do you remember who you were before realizing you've been living in an emotionally abusive relationship? That might seem like a lifetime ago. But try. Remember.

What might your friends have said about you? Maybe they would have said things like, "You were so carefree and full of life." Maybe they would have said, "You were full of dreams and never let anything get in the way of them."

Whatever they would have said, reflect on who you were before the abuse and spend time re-membering (reattaching) those character traits. They are still alive within you and starving for attention.

Thankfully, you don't have to continue to struggle as a victim of abuse. You can overcome abuse and thrive once again. You can be victorious—a surviving, thriving, liver of life. Dr. Steven Stosny encourages this in his article "Emotional Abuse (Overcoming Victim Identity)."

> Once emotional abuse occurs in a relationship, it becomes necessary not only to stop the abuse but to overcome victim identity through a strong identification with your inherent strengths, talents, skills, power, and appreciation of the self as a unique, ever-growing, competent, and compassionate person. This is accomplished through an emphasis on healing, growth, and empowerment, not by reviewing checklists of behaviors that qualify you as a victim or by reading lengthy descriptions of resentful, angry, or abusive behavior and attitudes of your partner.[6]

Wait a minute. This book is at least partly comprised of checklists of behaviors of abusive mates. Dr. Stosny, however, has a point. These lists are only helpful if they bring you clarity about what you no longer will tolerate in your life. They are only helpful if they lead you to understand what you are experiencing so that you can name it, validate it, and then move forward.

Moving forward means remembering where you were before the abuse began. It means tapping into your inherent strengths that you desperately need to carry you forward. You must learn about the pain in your heart, to be sure, but then you must learn ways to heal from that pain.

You have undoubtedly lost much in your painful journey, but you have not lost your core value. The psalmist's words are true for each of us.

> For you created my inmost being; you knit me together in my mother's womb. I praise you because I am fearfully and

> wonderfully made; your works are wonderful, I know that full well. My frame was not hidden from you when I was made in the secret place, when I was woven together in the depths of the earth (Psalm 139:13-15).

Re-member—reattach yourself to that part of you that was wonderfully made years ago. Clinging to these truths will bring needed strength for your healing journey.

Reclaiming Your Life

It is time for you to reclaim your life. Whether times of thriving were two or twenty-two years ago, it's not too late to begin living life again.

You *can* reclaim your life. In many ways your life has been taken from you. However, you *can* take it back. You can grow larger, more self-assured, more into who God made you to be. To do so requires courage and change.

You must seek to reduce and eliminate cognitive dissonance, brain fog, and the other abuse symptoms that reduce your personhood. You are unique, a one-of-a-kind person who cannot be replaced or duplicated.

To be fully and perfectly you will require receiving validation for what you have experienced. You will get that by reading this book, talking to others with similar experiences, and discovering friends who really know how to be a friend.

When you find your safe place, you must tell your story. You may begin doing this with a specialized psychotherapist who understands narcissistic and emotional abuse. You may decide to tell your story on the pages of a special journal. Offer yourself the unconditional positive regard and validation you deserve. Begin to experience empowerment as you move through the emotions associated with your losses. When you grieve your losses, you begin the healing process. You continue your healing when you sit with an understanding soul who grieves with you.

Then move from small to tall. Reenter life. Move from withdrawn to engagement in life and share your incredible story. Define yourself not by your pain but by your courage and the process of reclaiming your life.

The Path Forward

We have talked about growing smaller because of narcissistic and emotional abuse. Growing smaller is the result of being repeatedly towered over, being told you were inferior, and having those feelings of inferiority settle into your self-identity.

We further explored the power of crazy making, the debilitating impact of brain fog, and how that contributes to the loss of your self.

Finally, we explored the path of reclaiming your life, not living as a victim but rather as one who embraces life and is empowered by it.

As we move into the final section of the book, "Recovering from Narcissistic and Emotional Abuse," we will see how change begins—with you.

Part 3

Recovering from Narcissistic and Emotional Abuse

10

Change Begins with You

Listen, I tell you a mystery: We will not all sleep, but we will all be changed.

1 CORINTHIANS 15:51

It was the perfect home.

Christie and I had spent time researching where to build our dream home. I studied precipitation maps and found a perfect location that caught part of the rain shadow, meaning we would get less than half the rainfall of Seattle.

Located on Hood Canal with majestic views of the Olympic Mountains, we were thrilled as we considered a new life with waterfront property. We imagined our lives filled with digging clams and beachcombing.

Christie and I spent hours with an architect designing our home, hoping ultimately to create a bed and breakfast. We pored over plans, week after week, settling finally on the perfect layout for a house and attached cottage. It even had a crow's nest for me to write in.

We settled into building the house, which became a bit of an undertaking. Building rarely goes as planned, and this project hit snag after snag with carpenters, electricians, and roofers. Two years later, after numerous delays, we finally moved in.

After getting settled, our home and cottage decorated beautifully by Christie, we were ready for business. We were prepared with a name—Hood Canal Guest House—and lovely brochures. We had even joined the chamber of commerce. All systems go.

The guests came and went, all delighted with Christie's hospitality and the incredible setting. I sat back with visions of a nice money-making venture.

Fast-forward a year.

"I don't think I'm happy having people come and go in our home," Christie said one evening.

"What do you mean?" I asked incredulously. "This is what we planned. You designed this house and cottage and wanted a bed and breakfast. This is exactly what you wanted."

"It's what I *thought* I wanted," she stated emphatically. "I'm just not so sure anymore."

"It's just going to take some getting used to," I said. "What can I do to help make it work?"

"That's the point," she said. "I don't think there is anything to make it work. I don't think I want to have a bed and breakfast anymore."

"Wow," I said. "This is not good. We have spent a fortune getting this place up and running, Christie."

"But I'm not happy," she said. "I want to move."

I was not pleased and walked out of the room. After a chilly evening, she approached me the next day.

"Do you want to talk about the house?" she said.

"Fine," I replied, still struggling to wrap my head around the possibility of having built a bed and breakfast and now Christie didn't want to live there.

We spent the next few months arguing, talking, arguing, and talking. I must admit I wasn't always pleasant about it. I didn't want to change directions. I didn't want to consider moving after saving money, spending two years building, and preparing to run the bed and breakfast.

Christie didn't sway from her desire. She wanted to move. She wanted to live in a much smaller home without guests coming and going. She wanted to live in a cottage. She didn't want to live at work.

I didn't adjust easily, but I did finally adjust, moving past my initial fears and concerns. I finally realized that change is difficult and requires compromise and struggle. I realized that facing truths, no matter how challenging they are, leads to ultimate freedom.

I'm happy (now) to say we live in a lovely cottage, half the size of our former home. We are both delighted in our lifestyle, the compromises we both had to make, and the adjustments needed to get here.

You are facing changes much bigger than mine, but you can do it. You know the difficulties of facing hard truths. Change requires us to let go of what we have and stretching toward what we want. If we do that, we can get where we want to go.

Let's work together and consider change. Let's understand the fear of making changes, the dread that comes with it, and the exhilaration of reaching the other side.

Stages of Change

During those times when I become critical of myself for my slowness in making change, I remind myself I'm doing the best I can. I've always done the best I could with the amount of information I had at the time.

Hindsight is 20/20 of course, and we can all second-guess ourselves over our past decisions with the knowledge we have today. It takes great fortitude not to do that and instead to look toward the future. We have today—that's all.

We can critically review whether we are living today the way we want, considering we don't want to look back with regrets. We all have the power to move beyond our past and into our future.

Of course, we must do even more than that. We must be intentional about how we move into whatever future we're granted, and that is what this chapter is about. We will learn as much as we can about our life, making wise choices that will bring us closer to the person God wants us to be.

Know that God wants you to thrive, not just survive. To help you consider how you want to move from victim to survivor to one who thrives, you must know how to change. To move from an abused individual to one fully engaged in life, you must reflect on the process of change. How will you most effectively prepare for the new life you can have going forward?

The way to make changes in your life is to first understand how change occurs. Marc Perry, in his article "Five Stages of Change Model: Which Stage Are You In?," lists five stages of change.[1] He has identified some well-accepted stages to change you can use to measure your growth. Consider where you are in the change process and where you'd like to be.

Precontemplation

People in this stage don't want to make any change to their habits and don't recognize there is a problem. They live in that nether world of denial, which aptly stands for Don't Even Notice I Am Lying (to myself). You have undoubtedly met people who live in this world. Seeing only what needs to change in others, never thinking there are changes to be made in their own lives, their myopic view makes them nearly impossible to be around.

Living in denial, of course, keeps you absolutely stuck. We can't change what we don't own, and we don't own what we can't see. We can't see what we are not brave enough to explore. Change requires the courage to open your eyes and look critically at your life. As long as you are unwilling to do this, positive change is impossible.

Having moved beyond this stage, I looked back at all the excuses I made for not changing. I remembered the blame I placed on my wife, failing to honestly look in the mirror and see my own behavior.

Contemplation

During this next stage, you weigh the costs and benefits of behavior and lifestyle change. Here you have the gnawing feeling that something needs to change, perhaps even noting your world is not working as you would like. You consider change, but this is not enough to truly make changes. People can remain in this stage for years.

I rationalized, minimized, and found creative ways to convince myself my life was working. I repeatedly lied to myself, telling myself everything would be fine in spite of Christie's protests. I used denial as long as possible, clinging to a life I wanted. I was afraid of change.

Preparation

People in this stage have made the mental shift and are ready to change. They've set an appointment with a personal trainer, psychologist, or nutritionist—whoever can help them reach their goals. They develop a concrete action plan and a schedule for carrying it out. They may even establish someone who will hold them accountable to carry out their plan.

In my case, a final convicting and convincing conversation with my wife nudged me over the edge. It was the umpteenth conversation, taking place after much damage had been done to both of us emotionally. Regardless, I was finally ready.

Action

In this stage you are engaged in the process of change. You are exercising more, eating healthier, or taking the plunge in setting healthier boundaries in your relationships. You have crossed the threshold. No longer paralyzed in denial and frightened about the prospect of change, you are excited about the new possibilities.

I decided to make the move. I decided having a happy wife was far better than living in that location. It was time for a new adventure. It was time for me to swallow my pride and face the truth of the situation. It was time to move.

Maintenance

In this stage you are engaged in successful, sustained lifestyle maintenance. You have blended positive habits into your lifestyle. You guard, manage, and maintain boundaries that took some time to set.

My maintenance program means I listen more to my wife. It means future decisions are made much more collaboratively and at times, in submission to her.

It's Really Up to You

Kathryn—Kat to her friends—was struggling to believe her life was her own to do with as she chose. Nearing 50 and feeling discouraged about the life she had lost, she felt like a victim. Trapped in feelings of helplessness for so long, deciding her future was really up to her was a challenging bridge to cross. She had tried to stir up the courage to make changes within her marriage but hadn't experienced significant results.

"How can you tell me I have freedom of choice?" she asked angrily. "That's easy for you to say. You haven't lived with an overbearing man for 25 years. You haven't been beaten down and had your life stolen from you."

"You're right, Kat," I said. "I can't really know what it's been like for you. I'd like to hear more."

"It's been impossible, like losing your life one inch at a time," she said. "There hasn't been a single day that I have felt fully encouraged to be who I am. I don't think you or anyone can really understand."

"I agree, Kat," I said. "I really can't truly understand. I haven't been beaten down for 25 years. I haven't had my life dominated. I haven't experienced long-term depression. But I have had some life experiences that give me perspective. I want to escort you across the bridge of change. Even though it's scary, it's worth the journey."

Kat lightened, perhaps feeling a hint of hope.

"I've been thinking about my options for a long time," she said. "I used to think I would be trapped forever, but I have a glimmer of faith. It has helped talking to you and some women who are reclaiming their lives. I have been part of an online women's forum that has given me some hope. It's still scary to think about major changes."

"It won't be easy," I said. "I sometimes think I make it sound easier than it is. Change is a process, with stages. Each stage has its own challenges. But others have made the transition, and so can you. Others have found a way to face their fears, become empowered, and revitalize their lives. I know you can too."

Kat seemed unmoved by my words. While I have fought my own battles, none seem to match the battle women face when trying to reclaim a life taken from them by a narcissist or emotionally abusive man. I reflected again on how exhausted many women feel and how the task of recapturing their lives can be daunting.

As challenging as they can be, we must all navigate our way through difficult changes. We dare not become too paralyzed by the status quo.

We must move through stages of precontemplation, contemplation, preparation, action, and maintenance. We all must face reality and take the necessary tasks before us.

"It is up to you," I said to Kat firmly. "You will have to seek supportive people. If you look hard enough, there are many who can give you support, applauding as you navigate the frightening process of change. But we can't do it for you."

"I know," she said. "I've thought about it long enough. It's time to take action, and I know the action I want to take. I want to leave Jed for a month. I want to give him some time to think about what I've been complaining about and am ready to insist upon. I can no longer live with his temper. I can't live with him overpowering me and stealing my voice. It has to change, and it's going to take me leaving for a time for him to take me seriously."

I was a bit surprised—she hadn't seemed ready for such a bold move. She must have been making unseen progress, tackling unseen hurdles, and readying herself for the action phase of change. Listening to other women talk about making changes had undoubtedly helped her.

"I have a sister in Phoenix who has been scolding me," she said. "She wants me to leave Jed and make it clear that he has to enter into counseling before I come back. She's been tough on me, and I needed that. I know I need to do this now. I'm ready to do it."

"This is a big step," I said.

"But it's time," she said. "I've got to do this."

"Okay," I said. "Let's talk about a few things you can expect as you move forward with this."

"Sounds good," she said.

Resistance to Change

Kat had obviously considered her earlier resistance to change. She shared that she had walked through her fears about what Jed was likely to do when she left. She had played the move over in her mind a hundred times and was prepared for any number of possibilities.

"He is not going to like this," she said. "First he'll be mad. Really angry. I'm not sure what kind of retaliation he'll take, but he'll do something. He might cut me off financially. I'm sure he'll tell our friends I'm the bad guy. He's going to get everyone on his side. Poor Jed."

"Yes. Many men make all kinds of threats," I said. "They usually make threats in an effort to regain control. When they realize that you are serious, that their threats aren't working, most relinquish control. Not without a fight though."

She nodded.

"I can handle it," she said. "He won't like it one bit, but I'm prepared to face his anger. It's not going to stop me. I've got my support group, and the women there are encouraging me. I finally have got a strong network of friends who will stand by me."

We discussed how it was perfectly normal for Jed to resist change. No one makes significant changes without some resistance. This is to be expected.

Resistance is a natural part of the change process. If you understand this and expect it, you are likely to tolerate the stress of it better. When you realize that you resisted change, you are better able to understand that he will resist change too. He has to go through the same process you have gone through. We don't leap into change. We inch into it, sometimes kicking and screaming. Why should we expect anything less from a man whose world is about to be turned upside down?

Kat and I discussed how her husband had to go through the process of resistance. Resistance—actually a stage of grieving—is a necessary step toward ultimate acceptance and change.

"He will have to see and feel that you mean business," I said. "It will be natural for him to resist your change and push back. It's worked before, so why not now? He'll test you to see if you mean business. Expect him to try to bargain with you, offering a token of change. At that point it is critical that you not accept anything less than what you need. You will never have more influence than when you leave and he is left floundering."

"What do you mean?" she asked.

"What I have seen thousands of times is that when women become strong and courageous enough to leave, their mate feels threatened and struggles to regain control. If they cannot regain control they may act erratically. Your husband may become angrier. However, when he realizes you are not going to back down, he will likely come to the stark realization that the only path is *through* the problem, not around it. The only path for him is to squarely face what you are insisting upon. Change. Now."

Kat sat silently. Her conviction seemed to crumble.

"Am I doing the right thing?" She looked suddenly scared.

She was going through very natural doubts and fears, reconsidering her course of action. Taking the leap of change nearly always comes with doubts. We cannot fully predict what will happen, and it's a lot easier to cling to the world we know rather than face the one we don't.

"I can't tell you what is right or wrong, Kat," I said. "You need to act on your own convictions. This is a time to listen carefully to the Lord and His promptings. Do you have peace about your decision?"

"I have thought a lot about the Scripture that says, 'The peace of God, which transcends all understanding, will guard your hearts and minds in Christ Jesus.'"

"Yes," I said. "That is a great promise."

"Do you think what I'm doing is sound?" she asked.

"Your path does seem very sound," I said. "You have thought long and prayed hard about this. What you have told me you want and need is healthy. I support what you are doing."

Kat had reached the point of no return. Though frightened and concerned, she was ready to move forward. She would never likely feel 100 percent certain of her decision. Who ever is? But she had reached critical mass, the tipping point, where she had to move forward.

The Fear of Change

Kat was in the preparation stage of change. She had gone through years of precontemplation and months of contemplation, and now she was in preparation and soon would be ready to move into the action phase of change.

It is not unusual, when facing monumental change, to fear unknown outcomes. We can control ourselves, but we can never control how another will act. While Kat knew Jed well, she could not predict whether he was going to fly into a rage, threaten to withhold money, or perhaps even use intimidation to get her to come back.

I've seen it all during my career. I've seen men become enraged that their mate would have the audacity to leave them. I've seen men bar the door, empty the bank account, and make wild threats to regain control.

I've also seen men attempt to negotiate a deal. They bargain, hoping that if they give a little, it will be enough. They offer to go to a little counseling. They promise to see a pastor, all the while trying to maintain control of their lives. Most *hate*—and I don't use that word lightly—to see their mate regain power over their life.

Abusive men have learned to use power in their lives. They have learned whom they can manipulate and who cannot be manipulated. Once they have garnered power, they resist giving it away. They feel threatened when their mate begins to take control of their life.

Many men view their wives' transformative actions as rebellion. Those especially steeped in conservative Christian beliefs may label this grasp toward freedom as rebellion against them and against God. They use Scripture to regain control, and in many situations these actions are effective. This kind of power and control often reinforces anxiety and fear in women trying to change.

When a woman does not back down, standing firmly with her convictions, most men realize they are facing a different person, one with much greater resolve, conviction, and courage than in years past. Ultimately, if the woman makes changes in a healthy and respectful manner, most men come face-to-face with their own immaturity. Not always, but often.

I'm certainly not saying men will give in to change without a fuss. But when faced with significant consequences, such as the ultimate risk of loss of their mate, many men agree to participate in a change process.

No More Victim

Kat was finally embracing change. She had turned the corner and no longer saw herself as a victim. For Kat to embrace change, she had to turn away from identifying herself as a victim and see herself as a survivor. She realized, as do you, that change was fully up to her. Jed was not likely to help her, and friends could be fickle. It was up to her. Are you ready to consider this path?

Sadly, if you have been victimized for any period of time, it is common to begin to identify with being a victim. As strange as this may sound, you may wrap your identity around being victimized. You may look in the mirror and only see someone who has been deeply hurt, having forgotten the strong fighter that is within you.

There is a unique passage of Scripture where Jesus gets angry. He sees the money changers in the temple and seems disgusted that they would defile the temple of God in this way.

His actions seem a bit surprising because in the Sermon on the Mount, He speaks out against anger. In fact, He says that someone with malice in their heart is like a murderer. How is it then that He allows himself to get so angry?

The answer is that He is righteously indignant. He speaks out strongly against something that is completely wrong. He will not stand by while the Pharisees take advantage of travelers and desecrate the holy place.

How does this apply to you? You too must protect your holy place. You are a temple of the Holy Spirit (1 Corinthians 6:19). You, like Jesus, must become righteously indignant toward anyone who would desecrate your temple. You must become a strong advocate of your self. You must stand up and protect your self.

Only after you access this place of conviction within you can you rise up and set boundaries. You must no longer tolerate abuse. You will no longer identify yourself as a victim, but rather as someone who overcomes adversity—a true survivor. Can you find that place of conviction? Can you envision yourself as someone worthy of respect, refusing to be abused in any way?

In the previous chapter, I asked you to think about who you were before the abuse began. That may have been so long ago that it is hard to find that person now. However, it is critical that you do.

The Power of Choice

Kat found that place of righteous indignation. Though frightened, she had a sense of conviction that her decision was right for her. She also understood that Jed had to decide for himself how his future would go. Would he remain stuck, or would he choose change?

Both Kat and Jed came face-to-face with one of the greatest truths of humankind: Each of us has the power of choice. Though facing change from different perspectives, both Kat and Jed had all the rights and responsibilities that come with the power of choice.

God certainly had a creative plan in mind when He gave humanity the power of choice. This is a profound opportunity.

Scripture clearly spells out the possibilities: "This day I call the heavens and earth as witnesses against you that I have set before you life and death, blessings and curses. Now, choose life, so that you and your children may live" (Deuteronomy 30:19).

Wow! We have the choice of life and blessings if we will only access them. To access that life, however, we must make wise choices.

Throughout history we have been given the ability to make choices. As we all know, we make good choices and bad ones. We make choices that lead to a healthy life and others that are destructive, leading to poor physical and emotional health.

The apostle Paul reminds us about the impact of our choices. "Whoever sows to please their flesh, from the flesh will reap destruction; whoever sows to please the Spirit, from the Spirit will reap eternal life" (Galatians 6:8).

This Scripture gives me both pause and encouragement. The apostle Paul is saying that if I make decisions based on my selfish, prideful nature, the results will be disastrous. If, however, I make decisions based on the work of the Spirit of God in me, I will reap eternal, wonderful rewards.

These words offer encouragement to take chances based upon this principle. You have the power to make good, godly, relational choices. God has given you the power to make decisions that will have long-lasting, life-enhancing consequences.

This is also where faith comes into play. If we truly believe in those words of the apostle Paul—that sowing to please the Spirit leads to reaping true life—we can move forward with confidence. During these very difficult times, as you make life-altering decisions, take confidence in knowing that you can make good, godly decisions that lead to a blessed life.

Seeking Wisdom

As you enter your season of change, I cannot emphasize enough the importance of seeking wise counsel. You cannot travel this path alone. Just as Kat had her sister and a support group to fall back on, so you need some people who will traverse this path with you.

There are a growing number of women gathering together to offer one another courage and strength. There is a groundswell of dissatisfied women who need one another and are ready to receive and give support. On nearly a daily basis women call me, asking for opportunities for support and counsel, and we have developed a comprehensive program of treatment and support to meet this need. The need for wise counsel and support is great.

Why is support so critical?

1. *You will face significant challenges.* Few can fully understand the challenges you have faced and will face in the future. While few understand the nature of chronic abuse, those who have been there can offer support that others cannot give.

2. *You will doubt yourself.* As you prepare to make changes, you will doubt yourself. Often your perpetrator will question your choices, resulting in you doubting yourself. Support can mitigate this damage and raise your confidence.

3. *You may be abused on a greater level.* As you make positive, critical changes, you may face resistance and perhaps even be abused on a greater level. Feeling threatened, your perpetrator may become even more hostile toward you. You must prepare for this, and support will help you set needed boundaries on this abuse.

4. *You will gain wisdom from others.* Others have been where you are today and can offer perspective. Others have faced ridicule, threats, gaslighting, and bullying, and they can share their experience, strength, and hope. You will gain wisdom from them.

5. *You need a circle of friends.* Finally, you can form a new circle of friends who know what you are going through. These friends, some of whom you may never actually meet, will share a comradery known only by those sharing similar experiences.

These powerful suggestions will lead you out of hiding and into the loving care of those who understand you. They will help you face your fears of feeling foolish, insecure, or confused. There are many ready and waiting for you to join them.

Giving Up on Black and White

Talk-show personalities (constrained to fit their conversation into a one-time, limited time slot) usually offer black-and-white counsel, suggesting there is a right way to do things and a wrong way. Many unknowing individuals do too. Job's friends were black-and-white thinkers. Your mate likely thinks in terms of black and white as well.

Most of your choices and critical issues will not be black and white. There are few circumstances where black-and-white thinking is helpful. Life is complex, and certainly your history of abuse has many layers. Be wary of those who offer simplistic, black-and-white answers.

Kat shared the following story with me:

"It took me a long time to realize there were no easy answers. Some of my friends told me to just leave Jed. They'd say that if he was that bad I should just get out. Then friends from the church would say I had no biblical grounds to leave him. It didn't matter to them how I was feeling or what was happening in my home. It made me crazy. I knew the pain and damage I felt. Their counsel felt really dismissive."

"Life is rarely black and white," I said. "I have worked with enough women and narcissistic men to know that your life is complex—and your husband is complex too."

"Yes," she said. "It's so confusing. Jed is not all bad, and he's certainly not all good. I'm not ready for divorce, but I can't continue with the abuse. A lot of people want to lump him and me into a black-and-white box, where answers are simple. I have come to hate that kind of simplistic approach to life. There are a lot of grays in this world."

"Yes, there are," I affirmed.

"I learned who understands and who doesn't by the counsel they give," she said. "If they offer me simple, two-step approaches, I know they haven't got a clue. And I don't want anyone giving me counsel if they don't understand emotional abuse," she said, agitation showing on her face. "I can't take it. It hurts far more than it helps."

"I couldn't agree more," I said. "I feel the same way about working with the men. If you haven't worked with these men, seeing both their strengths and weaknesses, then be careful what you say."

Kat nodded.

Living in Ambiguity

I have a confession to make at this point in the book. I'm not always sure about what I'm talking about.

Like those I counsel, both men and women, I live with ambiguity. I live with grays rather than blacks and whites. I'm not always sure about the best course of treatment. I'm not always 100 percent certain whether to encourage a woman to stay and see if he changes or run for the hills to find peace and sanity.

I'm just not sure.

You know the feeling. You're not always sure either.

I recently received a scathing email from a narcissistic man I'd counseled. He was angry about the work I'd done with him. He challenged my work with him and the way I'd confronted him. He didn't like the confrontation and felt I'd sided with his wife.

This broken rapport adds to my feelings of ambiguity and uncertainty.

It is tempting to say he is the only one to blame. I'd like to say his criticism of me must have been completely born out of a narcissistic wound from my confrontation. Perhaps it's true. Perhaps not.

He is wounded, to be sure. I may never know exactly why. I feel self-doubt. I thought I did good work and thought we had a good rapport. I did confront him on a number of fronts, however, and he is very unhappy with me.

Was I too tough? Was I disrespectful at some level? Did I press in too hard or step on his toes too rigorously? I'll never know. I live with uncertainty and ambiguity. Can you relate?

You probably doubt yourself too. You too probably wonder if you have pushed too hard or tiptoed too long. You know the feeling of wondering about your choices.

Your path of healing, and mine for the work I do, must include an ability to accept ambiguity. Our paths are not paved and smooth. They are rough and rocky, rutted and strewn with debris.

Savoring Moments of Peace

Scripture tells us, "You will know the truth, and the truth will set you free" (John 8:32).

I've always wished this verse added, "But not before going through struggle."

Yes, that's more like it. Freedom isn't the only thing you will experience from the truth, but also angst and anxiety. Ask Kat if she is feeling free as she prepares to leave her husband to stay with her sister. Ask me if I felt freedom as I prepared to leave the home I loved for an uncertain change.

So, what do we do? We savor moments of peace. What do I mean by this? I mean that we must vigorously seek places of peace. Those places and moments will be different for everyone.

These moments of peace bring clarity—a respite from the storms of relationships. They allow us to feel God's presence, sensing whether we are moving in the right direction. They bring conviction about needed change.

I find comfort in reciting Psalm 23: "The LORD is my shepherd, I shall not want. He makes me lie down in green pastures; He leads me beside quiet waters. He restores my soul" (verses 1-3 NASB).

Ahhhh.

This was the passage of Scripture I chose to meditate on for several days during a quiet retreat some years ago. Sitting alone in an austere room with only a bed and desk, I sat quietly hour after hour. Free from electronic devices or connections to the outside world, I retreated. Just God and me, seeking peace together.

What are those moments and places for you? Where are the places that restore your soul? Some people find God in the mountains, while others are water people. Some find peace in a gathering of like-minded friends, and others gain respite by being alone. It doesn't matter what your place of peace looks like—only that you find it.

The Path Forward

We have talked about how change begins with you. We've seen that you have the power and responsibility to make your own choices and that those choices will bring life and health or challenges and difficulty.

These are strong words but true. This is your one, beautiful life, and you can make anything of it. If you embrace the adversity you have experienced, you can use it to make yourself stronger. None of your troubling experiences have been wasted. You are stronger and wiser than you were in the past. You are ready for change.

Perhaps the most important concept of this chapter has to do with attitude. You can choose to no longer identify with your pain, as great as it has been. You can now identify with strength, conviction, and positive change.

How will you choose? You are different now than you were when you began your healing journey. You are stronger, wiser, and better equipped to make changes. You can do it.

Now let's find out how you can embrace truth and allow it to set you free.

11

The Truth Will Set You Free

A lie can travel halfway around the world
while the truth is still putting on its shoes.

MARK TWAIN

It will forever be in my wife's mind as the worst sailing adventure ever. Not just a series of mistakes on my part, but a colossal failure that placed both Christie and me in peril.

Armed only with arrogance and pride, I figured I didn't need to understand compass navigation, maps, boat mechanics, tides, and currents or distances to move my new sailboat from Olympia to Harstine Island in the south Puget Sound. I figured navigating on water was just like navigating on land. Right?

Wrong! Wildly foolish and even reckless.

On a cold day in November, I coaxed my wife out of our warm home into a chilly car and finally into our freezing 25-foot sailboat. We had to wait a couple hours to leave because there was ice on the water in the cove where the boat was moored.

"Are you sure you know where we're going?" Christie asked anxiously. "I don't feel good about this."

"Sure," I said. "We're heading north, turning right, and then navigating around Harstine Island. We should be able to get to Jarrell's Cove before dark."

"Are you sure?" she again asked, distrusting my glib response.

"Yes, babe," I said. "I know what I'm doing."

In retrospect, this was a lie. It was self-deceit of the highest order. I cultivated an attitude that served only myself. I was reckless, foolish, and prideful.

My confidence heading out of the Olympia harbor quickly gave way to mild panic I did not want Christie to see. My boat plowed through the water at a sluggish five knots per hour, far below my original calculations. Rather than taking two hours to get out into open water, it took four. I was behind schedule from the start.

Any experienced sailor knows exactly how much gasoline they have on board. They know exactly where all the harbors are to refuel. They know the distance to the destination. They understand their charts and are prepared for a variety of dangerous possibilities that might occur.

I knew none of those things. My preparation was stubborn determination, ignorance, and magical thinking—not a good combination for a difficult navigation.

Needless to say, we motored well into the night. Christie became rightfully annoyed. Only after my ignorance was totally apparent did I admit to Christie that I was unsure where we were. There were no neon signs on the water directing us, no warning lights on land to guide us. We were cold, tired, and hungry, and I was afraid of running out of gas.

With a bruised ego, I prayed. Fortunately, God was with us. After motoring all day and into the night, we accidentally landed upon a buoy where we moored. When the sun rose the next morning, I was able to figure out our position and motor to a safe ending.

We no longer have a sailboat.

What is the moral of my story? Ignorance and stubborn pride nearly caused a disaster for Christie and me. Facing the truth of the situation from the beginning would have set us free from near calamity. It's critical to have the right information to make the right decision. The truth—knowledge about navigation—would have created a much more pleasant journey.

So it is for you. Believing lies spells disaster for you, but the truth will set you on the right course for healing and well-being. However, you must first be willing to face the truth. You must look deeply and courageously into yourself for any deception or misguided feeling. The truth will set you free only if you face it and embrace it. That is what this chapter is about.

The Lies You Believe

Believing what we want to believe feels good, but it does not help us. We may temporarily convince ourselves of something, but in the end this denial of truth only hurts us.

Though you and I have likely never met, there is something about you that I already know: You are tempted to believe lies. You convince yourself of things that are not true. You see a shred of evidence and believe it to be the whole truth. How do I know this?

I know this because you cannot live with a narcissistic and emotional abuser without being indoctrinated into his "spin." Remember that emotional abuse is largely a defensive effort at self-protection, filled with lies. He lies to himself and to you.

I also know this because you would not be reading this book and seeking healing if you weren't following a path of pain. You have been deceived and must now face truth. And not just one truth, but perhaps many different truths.

Before you can face the truth, however, you must admit to believing lies and learn to fully understand them. With that, let's consider some of the common lies abused women believe.

You Should Be Ashamed

Aubrey Sampson, in her article "The Most Dangerous Lies Women Believe," says women struggle with two main lies—that they aren't sufficient, and that they should feel ashamed of themselves for something. She shares that many women struggle constantly with the shame-based feeling that they should be something other than who they are.[1]

Just as Adam and Eve hid their shame behind fig leaves, so many women continue to hide parts of themselves, believing the lie that part of them is too shameful to be revealed.[2] This has certainly been what I've seen with the thousands of abused women I've counseled. They hide the fact that they are in an abusive relationship, which further intensifies their feelings of shame, creating a vicious cycle. Shame causes hiding and hiding causes shame.

It has been said that we are only as sick as our secrets. Just as shame gains power in hiding, shame begins to dissipate when brought into the light of God's truth. By owning shameful feelings and sharing them with others (along with other secrets you've been keeping), and by inviting God in with truth, you break the power of shame. To experience truth, however, you must be courageous enough to expose your shame.

Herein lies the power of support. As we express our vulnerability and shame, the secrets become open to truth. Allowing other women to speak into your life will bring incredible healing. Lies cannot exist next to the truth. When we bring our shame to God, He transforms it into radiance (Psalm 34:5).

This Is As Good As It Gets

Here's another lie many women believe: If you temporarily separate from an abusive man, you and your children will suffer endlessly. While certainly any separation will cause distress, staying with an unchanging, narcissistic, and emotionally abusive man will cause greater harm.

The truth is that appropriate help and support are available, and with them, you will rebound. The separation may also be the impetus he needs to change. So don't be paralyzed by fear, but rather take courage and immerse yourself in truth.

You Got What You Deserve

A final lie I want to discuss is that you don't deserve to have your own ideas or preferences. Of course, most abusive men won't admit to being controlling. They will rarely own that they talk over you, but they do. They rarely admit being defensive, but they are.

He says he wants you to think your own thoughts, to have your own preferences. But when your preferences come face-to-face with his, his will win out every time. Subsequently, you feel smaller, and the only way to regain yourself is to rediscover who you are and cultivate your sense of self.

All this may sound terribly selfish. It isn't. In fact, your life is both connected to him and separate from him. Yet you are responsible for caring for your self, and this is healthy.

Gullibility

Cynthia was an accomplished musician, playing violin for a major city orchestra. As if that were not enough, she also practiced law part-time. Additionally, she and her husband, Daniel, were raising eight-year-old twin boys and were active in their church.

To say that Cynthia had her plate full would be an understatement. Still, she appeared to do it all with relative ease. She had always been a high achiever, and her life reflected that. It looked to everyone who knew them that she had the perfect life.

Not all was going smoothly, however. Her marriage was slowly disintegrating. She hadn't even realized when she'd begun spending less time with her husband and more time at her other activities. She came to see me because she noticed herself becoming increasingly unhappy in her marriage. She had asked her husband to join her in counseling, but he'd refused.

"It's hard for me to be here," she said. "I've always prided myself in being able to handle things. I was taught to be in control of my life and my emotions."

"Well," I said after hearing about parts of her life, "you've certainly done that. What isn't working?"

"I feel myself slipping away from Daniel, my husband," she said. "I'm not even sure I love him anymore. We do fine raising our sons and being involved in our community. But I don't feel close to him. I suppose this sounds foolish."

"No, it doesn't at all," I said. "Tell me more about your marriage."

"There isn't really much to tell," she said. "He annoys me and sometimes scares me. He's always irritable, demanding, and selfish. I can't stand it. Originally I thought he would grow out of it, but that hasn't happened."

"Grow out of it?" I asked.

"I know that sounds strange," she continued. "Yes, I thought he would grow up. He's like a third child. His temper tantrums are worse than our boys'. He barks at me when he's upset. He embarrasses me. I hate it. I thought he would stop it at some point."

She paused and seemed to consider what she was saying.

"I assumed he would see how badly he behaves and just stop it," she said. "I guess that was naive on my part. Now I tiptoe around him. Or even worse, I avoid him and stop relating to him. Am I fooling myself about this relationship working?"

"Possibly," I said. "Men will act immaturely if they can. They often continue with bad behavior if they get away with it. Not all men, mind you, but many. What have you done to indicate your unhappiness?"

"Nothing," she said. "I just take care of things. I don't want other people to see what's going on. I overfunction and he underfunctions. But I'm feeling resentful, gullible, and taken advantage of."

"Yes," I said. "That seems to be the theme of your marriage."

Codependency

Can you sense the lies Cynthia has been telling herself? Can you see how she has painted herself into a corner and has taught Daniel that he can mistreat her? Of course, that was not her intent but rather a result of her own fears and codependency.

Cynthia seemed to overfunction and act codependently—losing herself to him, becoming smaller as he became larger. She overfunctioned by carrying the weight of responsibility in her marriage while Daniel acted immaturely. She was functioning codependently by avoiding these issues rather than facing them, and it was beginning to take an enormous toll on her.

Here's a good definition of codependency: seeing a weakness in another and ignoring it, thereby enabling and reinforcing it.

Let's break this down, one part at a time, and consider how your life may be impacted by codependency.

Seeing a weakness but ignoring it. When Cynthia was brutally honest with herself, she admitted she was ignoring Daniel's immaturity. Deep within she secretly knew she was putting up with behavior she loathed. She knew she was tolerating behavior that was belittling to her. Yet for complex reasons, she ignored these truths.

Enabling that weakness. Ignoring these truths caused Cynthia to enable his weaknesses. She feared intervening and doing her part to bring an end to his abusive behavior. She enabled his abusive behavior primarily because of fear that something worse would happen to her.

Reinforcing that weakness. Seeing his weaknesses and ignoring them, thereby enabling them, led to reinforcing them. Cynthia was actually creating space for her husband's abuse to become even stronger and more egregious. Certainly this was not her intent, but it was the result.

Healing for Cynthia required seeking truth, letting go of codependency, and finding freedom. She had to find and honor her self again, becoming the woman God destined her to be. Can you relate?

The Power of Collusion

Collusion is a process very similar to codependency. Collusion, when used in psychological or relational situations, occurs when two people tacitly agree not to talk about a prohibitive topic. Collusion exists in many abusive marriages—couples often refuse to talk about important issues permeating their relationship.

Collusion may begin innocently enough, as it did in Cynthia's life. It begins with a fear of talking about difficult issues, but it grows and solidifies as the couple continues to avoid difficult issues. There are often serious consequences to avoiding those challenging topics.

Consider what Cynthia had to say:

"I rarely confronted Daniel about his temper, but he knew I noticed it. I avoided confronting him about his controlling behavior and my fear of talking to him about it. He knew I was pulling away from him emotionally but never really said anything about it. As long as his sexual needs were met, he didn't seem to push for emotional intimacy. After a while he didn't even push for sex anymore. He has to know we are in trouble, but he doesn't bring it up, and neither do I."

Cynthia's story is one I've heard so many times. Women are often keenly aware of problems within the marriage, but they are afraid to confront those issues. They fear making matters worse. They fear being further abused. They fear being intimidated and threatened, choosing instead to cling to the life they have grown accustomed to. They trade a life of unknowns for what they know.

Collusion, for many women, is a strong but subtle process. Many are not aware they are giving their power away. Many come to believe they don't have many choices, so they settle into believing their dire situation is irremediable and accept it. They believe they truly are powerless, and they have long since given up any hope of talking about changing their situation or attempting to transform it.

Abusive men have various reasons to collude with their wives. In many ways life is working for them. Their power and manipulation work to get them what they want. The power and control become second nature to them. They have largely been successful at silencing the earlier cries of their mates. Life for them is what they want, and it's working for them.

You, however, don't need to continue getting caught up in his power plays. You can take a stand against it. No longer mesmerized and with a heart of conviction, it's time to dedicate yourself to healing.

Do You Want to Be Healed?

Amid your codependency—a common problem of losing your identity to another and very common with abuse victims—in the quietness of your heart you undoubtedly ask yourself some form of this question: "Do I really need change?"

Or you may wonder, "How much change do I need?" These are critical questions to ask yourself. What changes must I have? How important is it for me to obtain these changes? What will my life look like if I don't insist on these changes?

There is a fascinating story in the fifth chapter of John's Gospel. In this story Jesus was at the pool of Bethesda, where the sick gathered in hopes of being cured when an angel miraculously stirred the water. The name of the pool gives us a glimpse of the power happening there. The Aramaic word translated "Bethesda" means "house of mercy."

Jesus arrived on the scene and noted a man who was ill and had been there for 38 years. Crippled and ailing, he had waited a long time, undoubtedly suffering the consequences of his illness—unable to earn a living, care for his family, or be an active part of the community. These issues, which you may feel to a certain extent, carried a certain stigma as well.

Seeing the man, Jesus asked what seemed to be a rude question: "Do you want to get well?" Instead of responding yes, the man said, "Sir...I have no one to help me into the pool when the water is stirred. While I am trying to get in, someone else goes down ahead of me" (verse 7). Can you hear his desperation and helplessness? He seems to be saying there is little hope for healing.

Winn Collier offers a summary of this story, titled "Do You Want to Be Whole?"

> There are many reasons why we find it difficult, in our broken places, to stay connected with our desire for something more. To hope for (to live with the deep desire for) healing can itself be an excruciating act...We often abandon our desire for wholeness because we are deeply afraid. While the reality of our life may be far less than what we had expected, over time we make a certain kind of détente with our brokenness. It becomes what we know. It's a fearful thing to surrender the security of the present (no matter how disappointing or painful it may be) for the uncertainty of the future.[3]

To hope for change, to lean into the possibility of change, we must not only face the truth of our situation but be willing to embrace that change. We must envision it, see it, and reach out for it.

For you, this means acknowledging how deeply you have been hurt, how much you are ailing, and yet continuing to reach for healing. It means being honest with yourself about whether you have given up on healing.

It requires even more than this, however. It requires, like the man by the pool of Bethesda, that you face the part of you that has given up on the possibility of change. You must face any resistance to change you may be clinging to. If you will do that, you open yourself up to the creative possibilities of change.

Seeing the Elephants

Healing from narcissistic and emotional abuse will require not only courage to envision and embrace change, but also a willingness to admit there are elephants in the room you've not wanted to see or fully acknowledge.

You cannot rid yourself of elephants—issues within yourself and your mate—that you don't name and effectively face. Let's talk about cultivating an attitude of seeing the elephants.

First, you must *feel your feelings*. This may seem obvious, but when we feel emotional pain, it is natural to push that pain away. This is especially true if that pain is persistent.

When you experience narcissistic and emotional abuse on a continual basis, and you have challenges in your life that demand your attention, it's natural to push those painful feelings away.

Additionally, attending to your feelings requires some degree of safety. You've been in an environment where your feelings were not honored. This has been part of the abuse. To heal, to fully acknowledge the elephant, includes finding safe places where you can feel what you feel. Owning emotional elephants means having friends and places where you are encouraged to feel your feelings and even where that process is celebrated.

Feelings offer us critical information. They tell us what is missing in our lives and what must be changed. For Cynthia, this meant feeling her feelings associated with Daniel's control and anger. Those feelings included fear, discouragement, and sadness. She had to reflect on how his actions impacted her, the residual toll his actions took on her.

Second, you must *honor your feelings*. As you honor your feelings, you will rid yourself of unhealthy guilt and shame. You tell your brain that you are strong enough to explore the trauma you have experienced. You tell your brain that it is safe to return to your healthy self and healthy self-expression. You are worth it.

I cannot overemphasize the power of listening to your self. Again, your feelings offer a pathway to healing. Listen for signs and symptoms of needing more attention, support, care, and possibly rest. Your feelings will offer much instruction about what you need and the direction you need to take in your life.

Third, *set goals based on those feelings*. It is not enough to know what you feel. You must listen to those feelings, honor them, create safe places to explore them more deeply, and then set goals based on them. Make your goals specific and actionable. "I will get involved in a support group within two weeks," or "I will take art lessons to cultivate my creative side."

The goals you set must have some emotional punch. They must resonate within you. If you feel them, embrace them, and get excited about them, you will be more likely to follow through with them.

Finally, *embrace the godly wisdom within*. Scripture tells us, "If you look for [wisdom] as for silver and search for it as for hidden treasure, then you will understand the fear of the LORD and find the knowledge of God" (Proverbs 2:4-5).

Isn't it good to know we can search for and find wisdom? This is a powerful way to face the hidden elephants we've ignored. With godly wisdom we will know how to deal with the challenging situations we haven't wanted to face.

Seeing elephants is never easy. We've all got them parading invisibly in our lives. However, we can face them and own them, creating space for healthy living.

A Curious Mind

There is no better preparation for facing the truth that will set you free than developing a curious, open, and receptive mind. Emotional health is largely based on being open and receptive to what is happening in us and between us so we can embrace that information.

We must be curious to understand what we are feeling and what those feelings mean to us. We must be curious as to why we do the things we do, both in healthy ways and unhealthy ways. We must always delve deeper, asking ever harder questions of ourselves to find more complete solutions to our problems.

Being curious about our feelings, motives, and behaviors is a potentially powerful journey—one that takes great courage. To go on this journey, you must be willing to face insecurities, weaknesses, and even harmful attitudes. You must be willing to see the part of your personality that is small and frightened, capable of making mistakes. You must be willing to see the shadow side of your nature.

Curiosity may also be instrumental in leading you to a healthier relationship. Curiosity can be the drive that causes you to ask how you arrived at where you are in your marriage. Curiosity prompts you to ask tough questions that lead to powerful answers. Brian Grazer, author of *A Curious Mind,* says,

> Curiosity is the spark that starts a flirtation—in a bar, at a party, across the lecture hall in Economics 101. And curiosity ultimately nourishes that romance, and all our best human relationships—marriages, friendships, the bond between parents and children.[4]

Curiosity—asking what is really happening—will lead you to knowing what you need to know to make your life bigger and better.

Seeing What Is There

Would have, could have, should have...we have all been stuck in that rut. We wish things had gone differently than they did, that things were different than they are.

Stella was particularly stuck in ruminating about a life not lived. Unhappily married to Thomas for 30 years, she seemed to regret everything about her marriage except her three wonderful sons.

"I'm angry that I've wasted over half of my life," she said with obvious irritation. "I've been married to a man I don't really like. I should have left him years ago, and now I'm not sure what to do. I'm annoyed that I am stuck."

"Why are you stuck?" I asked. My question seemed to further annoy her.

"I'm 50 years old," she said sharply. "I'm not a young woman, and if I did leave Thomas, any man my age is looking for a woman 20 years younger."

"So you regret having stayed with your husband?" I asked.

Again she seemed annoyed. "Heavens, yes," she said. "I've wasted my life. I wish so many things were different. I wish I were younger, that I had more money, and that life was different."

"I hear your deep regrets and lost opportunities, Stella," I said.

I could see her sadness as she spoke.

"What about facing your life and considering what you can do with the life you have?" I asked. "Is it possible that you have more options than you think?"

"I can't see how that could be true," she said. "I've thought over my life from every possible angle. My life is a mess, and I'm a mess. I'm not even sure talking to you about it is going to change anything."

As I listened to Stella, I was struck by her resentment. Was her life really wasted? Did she really have nothing to look forward to? Were her choices as limited as she said? I don't think so. In fact, healing comes with facing life as it is, facing truth in whatever form it presents itself, and moving forward from there.

One of the most powerful tools available to Stella was to face her life honestly. Only in facing the truth of her life and facing real options could she move forward. An answer to changing her perspective was to actually see more—not only to face what was obviously there in her life, but also to open her eyes to seeing what she might be missing.

It has been said that what we pay attention to grows larger in our lives. If we focus on resentment and lost opportunities, our grief and resentment grow. However, those who pay attention to spaces and places of gratitude tend to be more satisfied with their lives. Those who open their eyes to new sights and sounds tend to be filled with new possibilities and hope.

Thankfully, there are usually many places and spaces of joy in all our lives that we miss because we are not looking for them. When we look for joy and reasons for gratitude, we find them.

I have been greatly impacted by the writings of Julia Cameron, author of *The Artist's Way*. Cameron says the answer to many of our problems lies in simply paying attention to life.

> The reward for attention is always healing...More than anything else, attention is the art of connection...pain is what it took to teach me to pay attention. In times of pain, when the future is too terrifying to contemplate and the past too painful to remember, I have learned to pay attention to right now. The precise moment I was in was always the only safe place for me.[5]

I love this idea. I tried to sell this idea to Stella, with some greater and lesser moments of success. I encouraged her to simply pay attention to her experience and what God may be able to teach her in these moments. As she noticed what actually existed, what was true, as well as what she might be missing—and be curious about that—she could lean into healing.

Embracing Truth Forever

"Life is difficult."

These are the opening words to Scott Peck's wonderful book *The Road Less Traveled.* I suspect his book gained a huge following because he had the courage to announce these words at the very start of his book. He could have been much more Pollyannaish in his approach, but he chose instead to say what we all know to be true: Life is difficult.

He follows this profound statement with yet another: "This is a great truth, one of the greatest truths. It is a great truth because once we truly see this truth, we transcend it."[6]

These are remarkable words. Is Peck correct that by embracing truth and the magnitude of our problems, we actually are able to transcend them? His words are similar to those of Jesus: "You will know the truth, and the truth will set you free" (John 8:32).

Was Jesus claiming that knowing the truth—Himself—would set us free? Certainly that seems to be the case. It is also possible that He was saying exactly what Peck was saying—that knowing and embracing truth sets us free.

People moan constantly about their lives, complaining about the enormity of their problems, believing life should be easy. Too often people complain about their lives more than they seek solutions. They complain about the unfairness of life more than they buckle down and change what they have the power to change.

It is undoubtedly true that we should spend less energy complaining about our problems and more energy solving them. We must take our precious energies and utilize them to make changes that enhance our lives.

That is certainly the message I conveyed to Stella.

A Path Forward

The truth will most certainly set you free, but only if you are willing to face it. You must look squarely at your problems—even the ones you would rather avoid or deny.

Now that you have committed to embracing the truth, you are stronger and better prepared to face challenges. Do you feel more courageous and willing to make changes to save your life? You have one life to save, and that is your own.

We are now moving forward and exploring how you can maintain dignity by setting boundaries in your life.

12

Maintaining Dignity with Boundaries

When we fail to set boundaries and hold people accountable, we feel used and mistreated. This is why we sometimes attack who they are, which is far more hurtful that addressing a behavior or a choice.

BRENÉ BROWN

In the beginning, God created the heavens and the earth. It was formless, and darkness was over the surface of the deep. The Spirit of God was hovering over the waters.

We will never know the exact mind of God, but clearly, He was not content to leave the formless earth alone. He immediately brought order and boundaries to the situation.

> And God said, "Let there be light," and there was light. God saw that the light was good, and he separated the light from the darkness. God called the light "day," and the darkness he called "night." And there was evening, and there was morning—the first day (Genesis 1:3-5).

And creation continued. God continued to bring order to His universe. We see order in His handiwork every day when we consider how all creation works in balance and predictability. As I look around and marvel at the mountains, valleys, moon, and stars, I think of Fred Hoyle's analogy:

> A junkyard contains all the bits and pieces of a Boeing 747, dismembered and in disarray. A whirlwind happens to blow through the yard. What is the chance that after its passage a fully assembled 747, ready to fly, will be found standing there? So small as to be negligible, even if a tornado were to blow through enough junkyards to fill the whole universe.[1]

I choose God. I choose balance, predictability, order, and boundaries—and that is what this chapter is about.

A Harsh Introduction to Boundaries

The book *Boundaries* by colleagues John Townsend and Henry Cloud has helped millions consider how they can apply boundaries to their lives. The topic of boundaries becomes even more critical and highly personal when it involves the issues of narcissistic and emotional abuse.

It wasn't a person who mistreated me, but rather a large corporation. It wasn't a single event that caused me to have vengeful thoughts, but rather a series of events. My nemesis was a cellular phone company who promised me a money-back guarantee on a phone, only to renege on their promise.

I had done my part of the deal, having paid them a handsome sum for the latest phone. I had gone over their guarantee in detail with them, making sure I would be satisfied with the agreement.

I walked out of the phone store with a smile and a new phone. All was right with the world as my yearning for the latest tech gadget had been satisfied.

My excitement, however, was dashed quickly as I discovered aspects of the phone I didn't like. Not one to make a hasty retreat, I decided to give my new relationship with the phone a few days to settle in, to see if we might grow in fondness to each other.

We didn't, and a few days later, still well within the guarantee period, I headed back to the phone store.

"I'm not happy with this phone," I told the stony-eyed clerk.

"What's the problem?" she asked.

"Not one thing," I said. "I just don't like the way the phone functions. It isn't what I hoped for. I'm going to shop for a new phone."

"Oh," the clerk said. "If the phone is functioning right, we can't take it back."

"What?" I asked incredulously. "I was told there was a money-back guarantee if I didn't like the phone."

"No," she stated bluntly. "There has to be a malfunction with the phone for the guarantee to go into effect. We would then offer a replacement."

"But that wasn't the agreement," I pleaded.

"I'm afraid it is," she said. "That is company policy, and there is nothing I can do about it."

"I'd like to talk to the manager," I protested.

"She's not in today, but I can give you her card," she said.

I took her card and made one final plea. "So there is really nothing you can do?" I asked.

"No, I'm sorry."

She didn't look sorry, act sorry, or seem sorry. I was annoyed, to say the least. I went home and complained to my wife, who offered sincere sympathies, having dealt with unscrupulous and dissatisfying phone and cable companies herself.

Over the next several days, I made phone calls and had lengthy discussions, but to no avail. My wife and I discussed our options and settled on small claims court. It would be David taking on Goliath, but that was how it had to be.

I spent days collecting data, preparing for court. I was sure of my position and knew I was in the right. Still, I was taking on a giant of a company that was not backing down.

To make a long story short, I remained convinced and convicted that this company should be held accountable to their policies. I decided I needed to fight this battle, preserve my dignity and boundaries, and proceed. Right makes might, right?

In the end, David won. What was important, however, was not the victory but preserving my dignity. I made another statement to those in my world about how I wanted to be treated. I recouped my money, chose a different phone company, and protected my boundaries—the theme of this important chapter.

What Are Boundaries?

There is a lot of confusion swirling about regarding boundaries. With everyone clamoring for their rights, healthy boundaries get lost in the mire.

Boundaries—markers of the space between where you end and I begin—are *not* what most people think about. We *feel* the impact of poorly defined boundaries. We *feel* the result of someone barging their way into our world or our head, and then we react.

It's time to stop reacting and to start methodically considering your values and what you want protected from others. Then you can get on with the task of setting and enforcing those boundaries.

Allow me to again define boundaries. I believe it is a very misunderstood concept.

Boundaries are what separate you from me. They are like fences that set you and what is important to you apart from me and what is important to me. You have your house and yard, and I have mine. I may invite you over to play—using the gate in the fence—and you may invite me over to play as well as long as I honor what is important to you. Boundaries—that fence with the gate—allow me to come and go and allow you to come and go with safety and dignity.

Townsend and Cloud note, "Boundaries help us distinguish our property so that we can take care of it. They help us to 'guard our heart with all diligence.'"[2]

Talking about boundaries is easy; implementing them is another matter. Depending on how you've been raised and the models you've had in your life, boundaries may not be part of your thinking and vocabulary. As a result, you may make mistakes like these:

1. *Failing to define your values.* If you haven't spent time reflecting on what is important to you or don't evaluate what you want protected, you are not likely to protect it.

For example, if having freedom to make personal choices is important, you won't know to protect that value. If you don't know that having some financial freedom of choice is important, you won't know to protect that freedom. You must take time to reflect and specify your values and what is inviolable in your life.

2. *Failing to define your boundaries.* Once you've discovered what is important to you and worth protecting, it is critical that you establish clear boundaries around those values. As has often been said, we teach people how to treat us. If you don't protect what is important to you, others won't either. You must take the time to share with others what is critically important to you.

3. *Failing to reinforce and monitor your boundaries.* Boundaries cannot be set once and for all. They must be continually reinforced, with consequences for violators. Others must learn we are serious about our boundaries. We will not be abused or mistreated, and others must respect us to play in our yard. We must reinforce and monitor our boundaries.

Making mistakes regarding boundaries is easy to do. Again, if you have not had a healthy role model showing you how to set and maintain healthy boundaries, the concept may be foreign to you. You may feel unworthy of defining and setting boundaries. Yet you are valuable and worthy of protection.

Donald Miller, author of *Scary Close*, shares the story of a workshop he attended where the presenter set three pillows on the floor. He had a woman stand on the pillow on the right, and he had Don stand on the pillow on the left. He told them they were both free to stand on the middle pillow because they had agreed to be in relationship with one another. However, they were never free to stand on the other's pillow.

Pointing to Don's pillow, the instructor said, "That's your pillow. The only person who gets to step on that pillow is you. Nobody else.

That's your territory. Your soul." The instructor then pointed to the woman's pillow and gave the same advice—that was her pillow, her soul. The middle pillow symbolized the relationship, to be shared.[3]

Boundaries are firm and strong, but like pillows, they're also delicate, soft, and tender.

Why Are Boundaries Critical?

Tamara came to see me following a very difficult separation from her husband, Tim. Married 15 years, she never felt the freedom to be who she wanted to be.

Tamara is 38 years old but tells me she still feels 18.

"How is it that I still feel so small and vulnerable?" she asked. "I'm a professional and have successfully raised three children. I've accomplished a lot in my life. Still, I've always felt under my husband's thumb. I've always felt insecure and frightened. I hate this feeling."

"Tell me more what is happening," I said.

"Tim isn't outwardly dominating," she said. "He just pouts or complains when things are not going his way. He has made me give up me in so many ways. What he wants has always taken precedence. I just finally got fed up and had to leave."

"What did you do?" I asked.

"I rented an apartment," she said. "It was tough, but I needed time and space to clear my head. I needed to learn more about what I think and feel without him telling me what is best for me."

"It is critical that we feel safe to be who we are, Tamara," I said. "That must have been very difficult to get that space for yourself."

"It was impossible," she said. "He threatened me at first, saying he wouldn't support me financially. I had to be prepared to make it on my own financially. He also threatened me with a divorce, and I had to be okay with that. He still is very angry that I left."

"How are you doing now?" I asked.

"I'm making it, one day at a time," she said. "I'm part of a codependency support group through my church. I've got some friends who are supporting me. I'm trying to decide whether to go back to him."

"I understand," I said. "I will say this to you. You have won hard-fought ground. It has taken a lot of strength to get to where you are. You must have changes from Tim. Don't give up that ground too easily."

"I agree," she said.

Emotional Abuse and Boundaries

Tamara is not fighting a normal battle. Hers is unique and more difficult than others'. Why do I say that?

Tamara is fighting years of oppression. She is fighting years of being told there is only one way to do things—his way. She is fighting the feeling of having built a fence over and over again to protect her valuables, only to have that fence kicked down.

Such an experience is more than disheartening. Such an experience steals one's confidence to keep trying. Yet like many other valiant women, she has clawed her way out and is now wondering what to do.

"I've learned that I can't fight fire with fire," she told me. "I can't outyell him or push past him. I can't intimidate him or outsmart him. I had to leave."

Still, in all of this, Tamara was able to find freedom, and she can now decide about her marriage. She has discovered what other women have discovered—the importance of stating her boundary and following through.

"I told him if he continued to disregard my needs, I was going to leave him," she said. "I said it many times when I didn't really have the courage to do it. But finally I was able to follow through. He's listening to me now."

Kellie Jo Holly offers this in her blog post "Personal Boundaries Are Important for Abuse Victims":

> A personal boundary is a rule that you say cannot be broken without consequence...The most important result is that you can now recognize abuse when it happens to you. After writing out even one boundary, you will experience the "red flags" popping up all around you when your abuser steps over your line. The red flags alert you to follow through with your plan—what you said you would do

> to protect yourself. You will feel stronger and your abuser's influence over you will diminish.[4]

Let's walk through some possible boundaries, clarifying your values and the consequences of violating your boundary. Consider each of the following statements, inserting your own value and boundary into them.

- "I value being treated with respect. If you call me names, I will leave the house and not return until you have apologized."
- "I value being heard. If you talk over me, I will bring that to your attention and stop talking until you listen fully to me."
- "I value being treated kindly. If you treat me unkindly, I'll remove myself from your presence."

Notice in each of these examples the importance of clarifying your values, stating the boundary, and then noting the consequence. Also note that when we set a boundary, we give up control of the outcome. We are simply announcing to others what we will do if they violate our boundaries.

Breaking Controlling Powers

Tamara has a job to do—to break free. This does not mean she has to divorce her husband, but she must break free from controlling powers.

Joyce Meyer makes a powerful statement about this:

> It is offensive to God to let other people control us. He sent Jesus, His only Son, to purchase freedom with his life...If you are letting someone control your life—intimidate you, manipulate you, and cause you to do what you know in your heart is not right—then you need to break those controlling powers. It is not God's will for us to be controlled by anybody except His Holy Spirit, and even that decision He leaves up to us.[5]

You can see in Meyer's words the importance of breaking free from emotional manipulation and control. Breaking free means taking the following action steps:

1. *Acknowledge your right and responsibility to manage your own life.* Yes, you have been given a life to manage—yours. Managing your life is not optional. You must manage it because no one is going to do it for you.
2. *Recognize when someone attempts to manipulate and control you.* Watch for the red flags of others attempting to think or act for you, telling you what is best for you. Notice when they get into your head and mess with what is important to you.
3. *Express your values.* Share with others what is important to you. Teach people how you want to be treated. Remind them of why something is important.
4. *Confront and set the boundary.* Confront anyone who violates a boundary you have set as important. Be very clear about why something is important, sharing feelings about being violated. Set the boundary with consequences for their behavior.
5. *Follow through.* A boundary is not a boundary without consequences. A statement made without consequences is a hope, wish, or complaint and will have little impact.
6. *Pray.* Bathe all of your actions in prayer. Make sure you are listening to God and following what He has designed as best for your life.

Some of these actions may seem harsh to you, but please remember that by setting boundaries we do our part to ensure our relationships are healthy. We must remain in only the relationships in which we feel respected.

Letting Go of My Life

We often think of setting boundaries as a way of protecting ourselves, and indeed it is. However, setting boundaries will also dramatically change your life.

Think about it. If you do what Tamara did—set a firm boundary with severe consequences—you will likely separate yourself in some way from someone you deeply care about. Tamara separated, literally and emotionally, from her husband. Where her path will lead is unclear.

In talking about a dramatic change in his life, William Bridges, author of *The Way of Transition*, shared the following emotional experience:

> I felt as though, like some latter-day Noah or Pinocchio, I had been swallowed by some immense whale of an experience. There in the darkness, I was cut off from all that I had thought was my life.[6]

Bridges captures the abject fear we feel when faced with making changes in our lives. In preparation for the massive changes he experienced with death and loss, he said, "We don't let go of anything important until we have exhausted all the possible ways that we might keep holding on to it."[7]

We've all been there—holding on for dear life, clinging to the life we know because we know it. We search out every possible option before embracing the prospect of change. Is it any wonder then that moving forward, even with newfound dignity and respect, we also feel fear?

Now that you are preparing, like Tamara, to insist upon change, you may feel even more fear. It's all right. Feel your fear and take steps forward anyway.

Insisting on Change

Unfortunately, setting and maintaining boundaries is not easy business. People are not clamoring to know your boundaries or respect them. Those who have abused you are focused only on themselves.

How then can you insist on change? Let's revisit Tamara's life and the path she has chosen.

"I journaled and talked in my support group for a couple years before I had the courage to leave," she said. "I laid out exactly what I needed and why I needed it. I reviewed my values, my boundaries, and what I was asking him to do or stop doing. But ultimately, I let go of believing he would change. That had to be up to him."

"What did you do next?" I asked.

"Nothing," she said. "Well, not exactly nothing, of course. When he pushed back again and again, I gave up. Not in a bad way. I just figured it was time for me to manage my life, not his."

"That sounds very healthy," I said.

Robin Norwood, author of *Women Who Love Too Much*, says stopping managing and controlling him...

> requires learning to say and do nothing. This is one of the most difficult tasks you face in your recovery. When his life is unmanageable, when everything in you wants to take over, to advise and encourage him, to manipulate the situation in whatever way you can, you must learn to hold still, to respect the other person enough to allow the struggle to be his, not yours.[8]

Yet your backing off must be balanced with pressing in. You must set those critical boundaries and hold to them. Then, after setting your boundaries and being perfectly clear how you want and expect to be treated, let go. Give him space to decide how he is going to treat you and respond accordingly.

Remember, insisting on change to play in your yard means insisting on change. Your message cannot be fuzzy or couched in too many "I hope" and "I wish" statements. No, it must be firm, clear, and precise.

"I told Tim that unless he sought professional help, I would be leaving," Tamara said. "Once-a-month counseling would not do it. It had to be with a professional who knew about emotional abuse. I interviewed several therapists so I would know who could handle someone like him. I told Tim I had a list of references if he wanted them. He didn't, so here I am."

How Much Change Is Enough?

Perhaps the most difficult question I ask victims of narcissistic and emotional abuse is, "How much change is enough?"

This always stops women, causing them to pause and reflect. I offer a bit of clarification. "Do you want minor changes, a little sanding off of rough edges? Or do you want significant change? Do you want him to fully understand the ways he has been abusive, take responsibility for those behaviors, and have a treatment plan for change?"

Their answer is always the same. "I want significant change," they say. "A little bit of change won't do me any good. I can't take anything but real change."

Okay. That helps clarify what they *don't* want—superficial, Band-Aid change. But it doesn't specify what real change looks like. It doesn't define and specify the change, determine how it will be measured, choose who does the measuring, and so on. More questions are raised than answered.

Lundy Bancroft has this to say:

> The tactic that the men we work with most employ to keep their partners waiting and hoping is to make minor changes. Ironically, the longer a man resists addressing anything that his partner wants him to deal with, the more mileage he can get out of finally making a little move.[9]

We still haven't answered the question, how much change is enough? That question is highly personal. I suspect, however, that by now you have a pretty good idea of what you need. If you are still in doubt, try this. Write out all the changes you would like him to make for you to be happy. What does he do that hurts you, and what would the opposite look like? Be specific and honest with yourself. Would you settle for less? Have you made these issues perfectly clear to him?

Change is difficult and challenging. Again, Bancroft helps us determine whether the abuser is really doing his work. Look at him critically and assess whether he has made the following changes:

1. *He surrounds himself with new, better influences.* You'll know

he has begun to change when he chooses to be around healthy influences. These, of course, can be found only in certain places—where healthy people congregate. (Or at least those striving to be healthy.)

2. *He's listening to you and valuing your opinions.* This one is so critical. You'll know he's getting better because he fully listens to you and deeply considers what you have to say. He recognizes your innate wisdom. He knows you're not out to get him; rather, you have his best interests in mind. In fact, he defers to you in many matters because of your wisdom.

3. *He takes charge of his life and his change process.* You'll know he's making progress because he has taken charge of his healing. You no longer want or need to have your hand on his back. He takes charge of his growth. He wants to grow and gets excited about going to church, support groups, and counseling.

4. *He has given up the victim role.* You'll know he's making progress because he no longer mentions the raw deal he's getting. In fact, he's happy changes have come into his life. Not only is he not a victim, but he's leading the charge to eliminate narcissistic and emotional abuse.

5. *He takes meaningful actions in support of your goals.* You'll know he's making progress because he champions not only his life but yours as well. He is interested in what God is doing in your life. He is excited to see you achieve your goals and helps you attain them.

6. *He demonstrates a commitment to long-term goals.* You'll know he's making progress because he is in it—growth—for the long haul. He's not watching his clock or calendar to know when he can stop meeting, reading, and growing. He is excited about change and welcomes feedback from you.[10]

Quite a list, huh? This may all seem impossible, but it isn't. Men who are ready to change, who have moved beyond the preliminary stages of healing, can actually get here. This list will help you determine how far he has come and how far he has to go.

Accountability for Change

The above list will help you determine whether he is invested in change. Even if he is invested in change, however, it is critical that he be held accountable to continue with the change process.

If he is invested in change, he will not balk at accountability. In fact, he will invite it into his life. He knows, as do you, that unless someone is watching over our backs, we can stray off the trail. We all need accountability.

Scripture tells us, "If you think you are standing firm, be careful that you don't fall!" (1 Corinthians 10:12). This warning is not meant to make us fearful, but mindful. "Be careful" is the admonition. Watch your step because it is easy to slip backward. If we aren't diligent with support, a clear path of change, and commitment to that change, regression is common.

I believe there are three important aspects to accountability—and this is another marker for determining whether you and your mate are on a path to change.

- *You have a clear goal.* You have identified what it is exactly that you are attempting to change.
- *You have outlined clear strategies for change.* You know exactly how you will accomplish your goal. The more specific, the better.
- *You have set a time when you will achieve your goal.* Setting a time line for achieving your goal keeps you on track. A goal with no time line is rarely achieved.

How does this apply to you? You will need to review your life and determine whether you have established clear, practical, and enforceable boundaries. If not, how and when will you do this?

Boundaries and Reparations

Progress, not perfection. That is our goal.

You are well on your way to understanding how you've been impacted by abuse, the tactics used by people who have abused you, and the steps you can take for healing.

There will be bumps along the way, and you need to know what to expect regarding making repairs when those bumps occur. Without repair, your relationship cannot prosper. In fact, intentional steps at repairing your relationship may disintegrate. Relapse is typically part of progress. Most of us slip back now and again. When we do, however, repairs must be made. Apologies must be part of any boundary plan.

When you have been violated, a sincere apology will include three powerful steps. It is critical that you expect and receive each of these three critical components of an apology.

A sincere apology. The violator must be sincerely sorry for what he has done. You will feel his heart of contrition. His remorse should be palpable if he is truly sorry.

When sincerely sorry, the violator should be moved with compassion. He will feel some of the pain of the one he has wounded. He will feel deep regret and remorse and will be able to show it to you. You should feel his regret.

Acceptance of responsibility. The violator takes full responsibility for the harm he has caused. He is willing to explore the depths of the pain he has caused. He reflects on the impact of his actions and listens intently as you share your wound.

When one accepts responsibility and the wide-reaching impact of his actions, the likelihood of the action being repeated is mitigated. A sincere apology, remorse and regret, and acceptance of responsibility for the harm he has caused is a powerful combination.

Appropriate amends. The violator understands that an apology is not enough. The past cannot be undone, but efforts can be made to ensure harm is not caused in the future. Efforts are made to offer restitution.

I recently met with a man whose wife left him because of his emotional abuse. He had traveled a long distance to engage in a two-day personal intensive, where I challenged him to dig deep within himself, discovering how and why he had been abusive. He had previously resisted change, leading to the separation. A central part of his work during these two days was learning the skill of making a sincere apology to his wife, taking full responsibility for all the ways he had harmed her, and mapping out his plan to make her feel loved and safe going forward.

Unless all three of these components are part of the restoration process, healing is not likely to occur. Again, the violator will want to do each of these steps well, knowing they are responsible for harm and to a large extent, for healing.

Freedom and Intimacy

Maintaining your dignity by setting personal boundaries has implications for us and those we care about. The process of setting boundaries leads us into an exciting place—freedom.

It is imperative that we all understand and master the art of setting and maintaining boundaries. In this atmosphere we invite others to be who they are and ask them to honor who we are as well. Many will appreciate our efforts to define ourselves and ask others to honor who we are, while many may not.

Jordan and Margaret Paul, in their landmark book *Do I Have to Give Up Me to Be Loved by You?*, remind us of some pivotal truths.

> We must cherish our individual freedom and be willing to deal with our partner's reaction to it—which is often pain, anger or indifference. And we must not restrict our partner's freedom...If I don't give you this freedom, my love is only a thinly disguised method for controlling you. When we care deeply enough for our partner to explore how he or she is affected by our behavior and to help him or her understand the fears that arise in the face of our freedom, intimacy deepens.[11]

This business of setting boundaries, monitoring them, and honoring others' boundaries is tricky. This, however, is where true connection occurs. We listen carefully to what others say to us. We listen carefully to who they say they are and what they say they need. If—and this is a big if—what they want does not violate us in any way, we honor their wishes.

This is our only true path to intimacy and healthy connection. This is our only path to being healthy individuals, capable of entering and maintaining loving, healthy relationships.

The Path Forward

Boundaries are an integral part of healing, and it is up to you to incorporate them into your life in a meaningful way. This is your one and only beautiful life, and you must protect it.

Setting and managing your boundaries is a fantastic way to monitor your well-being, because we are typically as healthy as the boundaries we set for our lives. If you are not feeling respected, review your boundaries and consider changes you need to make. If your life is going well, you are likely setting, managing, and protecting your boundaries.

We are now heading into the final chapter of the book, "Rediscovering Your Godly Self." I'm excited to share this information with you.

13

Rediscovering Your Godly Self

You've got to find yourself first.
Everything else will follow.

CHARLES DE LINT

Jill is a unique woman. She is amazing in many ways. She chose to stay in her marriage to Todd, who has a history of emotional abuse.

You might think Jill is weak, afraid, and confused. You might think she is in denial, pushing away the traumatic realities of her life. You would be wrong. She is anything but weak, afraid, or confused. She is clear, strong, and determined.

Jill is different from many women who come to see me. She has a spark I cannot define. She is sure of herself even in a chaotic world. Most would crumble under similar circumstances.

How did this 40-year-old woman get to this landing place?

"I spend a lot of time praying and reading, and I get a lot of support," she told me. "I've watched videos and really explored this issue."

"And?" I asked.

"I'm not sure about the future. Todd has been going to counseling for six months and seems to be changing. He has slips, but generally I see progress. At least enough to make me want to stay."

"How did Todd happen to enter counseling?" I asked.

"Not easily, I can tell you that," she said. "We had years of difficulty. We'd go to see one counselor after another, and nothing changed. I guess that happens to a lot of abused women. I kept persisting, and it wasn't until I separated from him for six months that he really decided it was time to change."

"And he's been changing?" I asked.

"Yes. He's in a really good group at our church and is in his own counseling. I see the counselor with him once a month. He's definitely working a program. I'm proud of him."

Still, Jill looked worried. "To tell you the truth, I'm afraid of how my future with Todd will be, but I'm sure I want to walk this out with him."

"So, how are you doing?" I asked.

"I have my good days and my bad days," she said. "Mostly good days. When he treats me with respect, I do fine. When he gets defensive, which is still a part of his personality, I have to really work to stay centered. But I've learned how to do that."

"Women who decide to stay with critical, defensive husbands have big challenges," I said.

"I understand that," she said. "Even when Todd is defensive, I watch for signs of progress and see them. Mostly, I have to remind myself who I am, why I'm staying, and what I have to do to ensure he is as safe as possible to be with."

"Why are you staying?" I asked.

"I've been given a ton of advice," she said. "Some people question me and tell me to leave. Others tell me I should stay. In the end, I have to decide. I'm the only one who lives my life, and I've decided it's worth it. He is a good man, and for the most part, I like my marriage."

She paused. "I don't think I answered you," she said, smiling. "Why am I staying? Because I believe we are working together to be healthy. He is doing enough to give me hope. I'm practicing setting boundaries, being assertive in a healthy way, holding him accountable, and remembering who I am. He doesn't define me. God defines me."

Her words echoed in my mind—"God defines me."

I listened carefully to her, still wondering how she was able to be so stable amid her challenges. How was she able to move from being reactive—reacting to the things Todd has done to her in the past—to being her own person, defined by God?

"Don't get me wrong," she continued. "I have days when I reconsider my decision. I'm still healing from what has happened. But for now, I'm choosing to stay and work on our marriage together. I'm choosing to work on me in my marriage, not away from him."

"I'm very impressed with your self-confidence, Jill," I said. "You have something a lot of women would like. You sound very clear and filled with conviction."

"Today," she said softly.

We continued to talk about what was helping Jill stay balanced while living in a marriage with problems. She shared more about her marriage as a place to grow and rediscover her godly self—and that is what this final chapter is about.

Crisis as Opportunity

This book has largely been about understanding the impact of narcissistic and emotional abuse. I have written from the victim's perspective. As I bring this book to a close, I want to emphasize that you are not only a victim, but a survivor—one who overcomes.

You may have related to the stories of courageous women struggling to heal from this abuse, so perhaps it will be a bit more difficult to identify with women like Jill. But she is part of a significant group of women who have chosen to utilize their marriage as their place to grow. Women like Jill see their marriage not only as a place of struggle and challenge but also as a place of opportunity.

Is it possible to heal amid the crisis? Is it possible to carve out a space where you can not only embrace and nurture your wounds but also thrive? Many women like Jill offer a solid yes.

When facing crises, we usually try to cope. We clinch our teeth, grip our chair, and hold on for dear life. We try to avoid crises because they are typically places of pain.

Jill would say differently.

"I'm viewing this as a time to grow," she said. "It is most definitely a hard time in my life. I'm not completely happy with Todd. But I'm leaning into the experience and trying to see what God has for me in it."

Consider some of the benefits of a marriage crisis.

First, *your world is shaken up*. When experiencing a crisis, the world we have known is rattled. We can no longer keep doing things the way we've always done them. We must change.

"I am so upset with Todd at times that I have to step back and look at things from a new angle," Jill said. "I can't live the way I've always lived. It's not working for me. My emotions are in an uproar, and I have to attend to them."

Second, *you can view your situation differently*. When our world is turned upside down, we have a chance to view things differently. We can look for the opportunity in the crisis. When our world is shaken up, we can let go of the known and at least take a glimpse of the unknown.

"I can keep complaining about my marriage," Jill said, "or I can decide what I want to do. I discovered I had choices. That was powerful for me."

Third, *you have an opportunity to change*. Relationships tend to continue in the same patterns unless we experience enough discomfort. When we reach the tipping point of discomfort, change is possible.

"I decided to be different in my marriage," Jill said. "I had focused on Todd changing for the longest time. I made a shift and decided I was going to be different and see what happens."

Are you a person who delves into a crisis to find the opportunity, or are you always looking backward at the missed opportunities? Your answer is critical and may indicate a need to change perspectives.

Being the Change You Want

Mahatma Gandhi is often quoted as saying, "Be the change you wish to see in the world." It's a great paraphrase, but here's the actual quote: "If we could change ourselves, the tendencies in the world would also change. As a man changes his own nature, so does the attitude of the world change towards him...We need not wait to see what others do."[1]

Rediscovering your godly self means envisioning who you want to be and then being it. It means believing that God still has a plan for your life and that you can discover it.

Perhaps I make it sound too simple, perhaps not. What if being your perfect self, the self you and God want you to be, means a change of perspective? Rather than focusing on your husband, you focus on you.

Henrik Edberg, in his blog post "Gandhi's 10 Rules for Changing the World," shares these provoking thoughts:

1. *Change yourself.* I've written that change begins with you. Now I'm adding that I want you to focus on changing you, not him. If you change yourself, you will change your world. Additionally, if you change your world without changing yourself, you will still be the same.
2. *You are in control.* You are not in control of everything, of course, nor are others totally in control of you. However, you control yourself and your choices. You control your thoughts, your actions, and to a certain extent, your emotions. As you change your actions, your emotions will change as well.
3. *Forgive and let go.* Scripture offers sobering counsel when it says, "If you forgive other people when they sin against you, your heavenly Father will also forgive you" (Matthew 6:14). While rarely easy, you can forgive others. This certainly does not mean allowing anyone to abuse you, but it does mean you let go of resentment in your heart.
4. *Without action, you aren't going anywhere.* Thinking, reflecting, and even praying are good practices. But action must follow. You must do something to become the person you want to be. Take a small step today toward becoming that person.
5. *Take care of this moment.* As tempting as it is to get ahead of ourselves, worrying and planning for tomorrow, we must stay in this present moment and take care of it. Make choices as to how you want to live in this moment.
6. *Everyone is human.* It is critical that you not hold others to unreasonable standards. Just as you want others to allow

you room to make mistakes, so you must allow others to do the same. As you reflect on their humanity, you may find more in them that you care about.

7. *Persist.* In time, as you change, the opposition around may fade. Certainly as you grow and become stronger and more resolved, others see and cannot help but respect these changes. Many will begin to accept this new you. While this is still not guaranteed, as you change you will begin to see others notice and treat you differently.
8. *See the good in people and help them.* We are all a combination of good and bad. See the good. When you see the good in others, you will be more likely to care about them and help them. Everyone is struggling a fierce battle and needs our help.
9. *Be congruent, be authentic, be your true self.* Your thoughts, words, and actions need to be in alignment. When they are, you send a clear message. When you know your convictions and live them out, others will hear and feel them and likely will come to respect them.
10. *Continue to grow and evolve.* You can keep growing. You have not arrived, nor have I. Have compassion for yourself and the journey you are on. Continue going to your support group and church, reading, and attending to other aspects of your recovery. Notice that he, too, is on his own journey.[2]

This is an incredible list of action steps to propel you in the right direction. Perhaps you can select one or two that really speak to you and make them your goals for becoming the best version of yourself—the person God wants you to be.

Giants in the Land

All of this may sound too easy, especially when there are those shouting that he cannot change or that you are a victim with few choices.

Your world may be filled with people who have victim mentalities. You cannot afford to indulge in that kind of thinking.

Rediscovering your godly self means facing opposition. It means listening carefully to those with experience in narcissistic and emotional abuse, but it also means listening to yourself.

There will always be people who tell you that you cannot reach your goals. That you cannot be a survivor. That the obstacles are simply too high, the challenges too great.

I've included some stories of biblical characters who faced opposition and overcame it. Moses was one of those individuals.

Moses was the leader of the Israelites. They constantly grumbled and complained even though they were promised a land filled with milk and honey. Moses captured the vision God had for His people.

One day the Lord spoke directly to Moses, giving him clear instructions. "The LORD spoke to Moses saying, 'Send out for yourself men so that they may spy out the land of Canaan, which I am going to give to the sons of Israel'" (Numbers 13:1-2 NASB). God, of course, knew what was in Canaan. God was testing Israel to see if they would have faith in His promises. God had already gone before them, and their task was to follow in faith.

Moses followed God's instructions and sent twelve men to scout out the land. The first report came back with ten of the twelve saying indeed the land *did* flow with milk and honey. They even brought back luscious grapes to show how plentiful the land was. But there were enemies in the land that were big and strong and mighty—giants!

Aren't these words reminiscent of those in our lives who spoil our dreams? We've all had people tell us we could not go where we wanted to go or do what we wanted to do. You've heard people say you cannot survive in the midst of narcissistic abuse. Even a small amount of abuse will completely stifle your growth, they say.

Two of the twelve men Moses sent out, Caleb and Joshua, stood up against the other ten. They admitted that indeed there were enemies in the land, but they said they should go up against the enemies because they would overcome them.

You know the feeling—taking a stand against others. You know when your optimism is faced squarely with pessimism. Ten of the spies didn't share Caleb and Joshua's optimism.

> They spread among the Israelites a bad report about the land they had explored. They said, "The land we explored devours those living in it. All the people we saw there are of great size. We saw the Nephilim there...We seemed like grasshoppers in our own eyes, and we looked the same to them" (Numbers 13:32-33).

Joshua and Caleb were not swayed from what they saw and believed.

> The land we passed through and explored is exceedingly good. If the LORD is pleased with us, he will lead us into that land, a land flowing with milk and honey, and will give it to us (Numbers 14:7-8).

The moral of the story is this: Discouragement is contagious. It is easier to believe you cannot do something than to believe you can. It is easy to slip into doubting what you have heard God say to you. Consider again Jill's words.

"I have a sense that I can trust changes are happening with Todd. He is working with a great group of guys, and I've even heard from some of their wives about good things happening in that group. I keep thinking about not being defined by others, but being defined by God."

Jill paused again. "I'm not saying my path is right for everyone, but it's right for me. The Lord gave me the Scripture, 'The LORD is my light and my salvation—whom shall I fear? The LORD is the stronghold of my life—of whom shall I be afraid?'" (Psalm 27:1).

To whom are you listening? Are people saying you should be afraid when God tells you to have faith? Be careful and be certain about which voices you will attend to. If you see enough positive signs to give you hope and give you confidence to stay, perhaps that's the right thing to do.

Marriage as a Place to Grow

Many like to tell me the only place they struggle in relationships is in their marriage. They share this with me as a justification for the problem being just in their marriage, not their personality.

It's not true.

I've been a member of that club—blaming my marriage for my irritable temperament—but I eventually realized I was being unfair. Truth be known, marriage is the place where our issues come to the surface. Our mate is the primary person who knows our issues.

Now, please don't read into this any kind of justification for narcissistic and emotional abuse. It is anything but that. What I'm saying is that you have an opportunity to step back and see what issues are revealed in your marriage. Marriage reveals issues more often than it creates them.

What if you viewed your marriage as a place to grow, not just as a place to cope? Again, please understand I don't want you to stay in an abusive environment where you cannot be healthy. What I am saying is that Jill's story is worth considering. Healing can sometimes happen in an imperfect marriage.

Let's consider how you would decide whether you can grow in your marriage. What are the issues to consider?

First, *can you be healthy in your marriage?* This is a critical issue. If you find yourself regressing, getting emotionally or physically ill, I don't believe you should stay with your mate.

Whether you are like Jill and choose to stay in your marriage or feel unsettled and emotionally challenged, you must be healthy. You have a responsibility to yourself, your children, and even to God to take care of yourself.

Second, *can you feel safe*? If you cannot feel safe, you cannot grow emotionally and be well physically. Feeling unsafe every day takes a tremendous toll. You must have some measure of safety to be the person God has called you to be.

Third, *does your mate take at least some responsibility for your welfare and the welfare of the marriage?* You cannot improve your marriage alone. You must have some degree of cooperation to have a healthy marriage, and your marriage must be somewhat healthy for you to be healthy yourself.

Finally, *does your mate allow you space to grow emotionally and spiritually?* He may not join you on your healing journey, but he must at least allow you space to grow. That means he must allow you to do the things that bring growth to your life, such as attend support groups, attend church, and enjoy healthy friendships.

If your mate supports your growth and is deeply involved in his own healing journey, it may be possible for you to remain in the marriage. In fact, if you can get healthy together, your marriage may be an excellent place to grow.

Self-Care Is Resistance

Finding an emotional and physical space where you can grow is critical. Only when you feel safe can you find a peaceful place to listen to God, healthy friends, and yourself.

Self-care is more than getting support, however. It is also taking a stand against what is wrong. It is about having convictions and acting on those convictions.

Mysia Anderson, in her meaningful blog post "Self-Care Is Resistance," says self-care is much more than intentional acts of kindness toward yourself such as taking naps, eating well, exercising, and stepping back from commitments, as important as these steps are. She says self-care is not only an act of love but a form of resistance.

> Living and surviving in the midst of scrutiny and violence is a radical act. Intentionally caring for your well-being, and making attempts to love yourself despite insults and dangers against your being, is a radical act.[3]

The concept of resistance may feel radical to you. It would be nice if we had a throng of cheerleaders to champion our progress, but this won't always be the case. In fact, it is likely you will feel painfully alone at times. Nonetheless, you must determine to follow the path the Lord has laid out for you. When you meet with those who doubt you and shout, "There are giants in the land," you must push back. You must resist and claim your identity. If you are certain of your path, hold fast to it.

Finding Meaning in the Struggle

One key to rediscovering your godly self is to find meaning in the midst of your struggle, not in the absence of it.

This is a powerful truth. Many of us wait for the struggle to end before moving forward with our lives. Complaining about the way life is, we tell ourselves we will take action and grow when it is perfectly safe to do so. However, history has shown that we must find meaning and make difficult decisions in the midst of struggle.

We have countless examples of people who have exhibited strength and tremendous courage when experiencing unspeakable difficulty. Abraham Lincoln, Martin Luther King Jr., Nelson Mandela, and countless others have risen above their trials to provide inspiration to us all. Of course, our greatest example is Jesus Himself.

Long ago, as a college student filled with angst, I discovered the book that changed many people's perspective on life—*Man's Search for Meaning*, written by Viktor Frankl in 1946. In it he chronicled his experience in the Auschwitz concentration camp during World War II. He wrote about how he found purpose in the midst of incredible suffering. He identified something in his experience that was meaningful and then immersed himself in that outcome.

Frankl concluded the meaning of life can be found in every moment of living and that life never ceases to have meaning, even in suffering and death. He said that a prisoner's reactions were not solely based on the conditions of his life but also the freedom of choice one always has in his suffering. He noted that suffering ceases to be suffering when we find meaning in our experience.[4]

What do Frankl's words mean to you? You have not been in a concentration camp, but you have endured suffering. You have likely questioned why you are in the situation you are in. Perhaps you've gone so far as to question God and wonder why you have not found a miraculous release from your pain. Know that there is purpose in your life, even in spite of your circumstances.

Chrysalis

I can remember the first time I read about the chrysalis. I must have been all of ten years old. I read with amazement.

How could an insect enter into a tiny case for months and go through a transformation, merging in the spring as a butterfly? This was impossible.

I read more. It was true. I took a keen interest and actually watched the transformation occur in nature. The caterpillar spun its chrysalis and emerged months later as a butterfly. The chrysalis has had special meaning for me ever since. I believe we all can enter a "chrysalis season" and emerge as butterflies.

Regardless of what happens in your life, it is imperative that you find your purpose—the transformation needed. It is critical to discover who God has meant you to be so you can enter a change process and emerge as something entirely new.

It is exciting to consider that you can discover your godly self regardless of what is taking place in your life. You may feel exhausted from your journey, but you still have a voice crying out to be heard. You have gifts and talents to share with others. There is a new you ready to burst onto the scene with bright colors.

Take your eyes off your circumstances for a moment. Reflect on who your godly self really is. Consider what moves you.

Are you moved when you hear a story of a homeless person being given food and shelter? Do you have an interest in helping those less fortunate than you? This may indicate a passion and purpose.

Are you moved when walking through an art gallery, viewing exquisite paintings and sculptures? Time seems to stand still as your eyes are affixed to the artistry before you. This may reveal some creativity within.

Are you touched when hearing Andrea Bocelli and Sarah Brightman sing "Time to Say Goodbye"? Perhaps music has some special meaning to you and signals something for you to attend to.

You may long to be wealthy and able to give boundlessly to others, or to be a painter, sculptor, or musician, but you can only be you. Still, you can be the best you possible. This means finding your voice, your artistry, your passion, and giving expression to it.

Finding Your Voice

Having learned that marriage can be a place to grow if there is a measure of safety, and armed with a new mindset, it is critical to add yet something more.

Stephen Covey, author of *The 7 Habits of Highly Effective People*, wisely decided there was an eighth habit needed for people to become all they were meant to be: "Find your voice and inspire others to find theirs." In his last book, *The 8th Habit*, Covey passionately says,

> The 8th Habit...is the voice of the human spirit—full of hope and intelligence, resilient by nature, boundless in its potential to serve the common good...
>
> The power to discover our voice lies in the potential that was bequeathed to us at birth. Latent and undeveloped, the seeds of greatness were planted. We were given magnificent "birthgifts"—talents, capacities, privileges, intelligences, opportunities—that would remain largely unopened except through our own decision and effort.[5]

This is so true. There is within us a God-given desire to be all we can be, to express the yearning to find our voice in life. We want to talk about what is happening within us. We want to be heard and to hear.

What is it you want to say? Who is it you want to be? If you are like me, you have a message you want to proclaim. You want to influence others in some way, be it with your music, your art, your writing. Perhaps it is with your service and acts of kindness for humanity.

As you use your voice and speak out your truths, you will grow. As you find your community of safety, your voice will become stronger.

Choosing to Leave, Choosing to Stay

As you find your voice and discover your ability to make choices, perhaps your greatest decision is whether you choose to leave or to stay. Perhaps you find you must leave to feel healthy and safe.

Perhaps your decision to leave will be permanent. You have tried and tried to single-handedly save your marriage, only to become more exhausted and weary. Feeling utterly abandoned and mistreated, you have decided you must leave.

Perhaps, like many others, you have decided to stay for now. Yet you recognize you must rediscover your passion for life. You must live, not just survive.

Perhaps like Jill, you decide to stay and to thrive. You have a sense you can be healthy even as your mate attempts to become healthy. Regardless of his actions, you have decided for a season you will focus on you and being the person God designed you to be. You will experiment with life and see where it takes you.

Townsend and Cloud, in their book *Safe People*, note that the key to deciding whether to leave or stay hinges on one last factor: Can the person you're with be safe?[6]

While they list numerous indicators of a safe person, one in particular stands out that I would like to highlight. Unsafe people think they have it all together rather than admitting weaknesses.

Becoming your godly self means being vulnerable, open to others, and influencing others. This cannot be done in a hostile, threatening environment. Consider once more what Jill has discovered.

"For me to stay meant having several very firm talks with Todd. I could stay as long as he was working on himself. I could stay as long as he gave me some room to explore myself, supporting my involvement in my groups and my church. Those were prerequisites to me staying. I didn't need him to be on the same path I was on, but he had to support my journey."

Notice Jill needed room to explore herself. This will be different for each person. For some it means an absence of crazy-making behaviors. For others it means knowing their mate is working to become healthy. For others it means simply being given the freedom to be on their own healing path without criticism for that journey.

What do you need to feel safe? What do you need to explore who God has designed you to be?

All Things Work Together for Good

You have undoubtedly wondered why you are in the situation you are in. Why have you not been miraculously freed? Like the man sitting by the pool of Bethesda, you may have wondered why you have not been healed. Why have your circumstances not changed?

I cannot answer those questions. What I can do, however, is offer hope.

The apostle Paul offers a most perplexing yet hopeful message when he says, "We know that in all things God works for the good of those who love him, who have been called according to his purpose" (Romans 8:28).

Does this mean that all things are good? Of course not. Bad behavior is bad. Hurtful behavior is hurtful. God never approves of abuse.

Yet there is a powerful and hopeful message in this for you and me. All things—trials, losses, suffering, mistreatment—can work together for good.

How can good come from mistreatment and abuse?

I have heard many testimonies from women in abusive relationships. They have shared with me that their suffering has caused them to reflect on God in a deeper way. Their abuse has caused them to drop to their knees in pain and search for God. It has caused them to critically review their perspective to see if there is something about themselves they need to change.

Mostly, these women have taught me the important lesson of trusting God to guide them. They have learned lessons of being joyful always, praying continually, and giving thanks in all their circumstances.

Love Does

You are in a less-than-perfect relationship. In the midst of this, I encourage you to embrace a truth: God loves you and encourages you to love yourself and others.

In Hosea 11 we read how God loved His children, Israel, even though they turned away from Him. While Israel kept failing, God kept loving. God is a loving Father who desires His best for His children.

This is a powerful image to bear in mind as you consider your situation and make critical decisions about your future. God persists in His love for you. God persists in offering you wisdom to make the very best decisions.

It is the dead of winter as I finish writing this book. During the many months of writing, a pair of eagles—whom I've nicknamed Jack and Jill—have been building a nest. Actually, they're building what appears to be a three-story condominium complex.

At times I've seen only one of them doing the building. I've wondered what happened to the other. Was he or she kicked out of the nest? Did they have a spat? Was there a divorce?

Sometime later the other would show up, often carrying another branch for the emerging complex. Did he or she arrive with this gift to repair a broken relationship? I don't know.

As of today they are together. As of today they continue building, each with respective responsibilities I don't fully understand. What I know is I have been shocked at their tenacity. They have worked tirelessly throughout the heat of summer, the cool breezes of fall, and now the freezing temperatures of winter. They never stop.

I've watched these majestic birds drag limbs ten times the length of their bodies through the air to their nest-condo complex. With talons clinging to their foundation material, flooring, and walls, they just keep building, creating a nest for love to continue.

I imagine Jack and Jill to be thrilled with their enterprise. Come spring, if all goes according to plan, they'll be raising a fine family on Puget Sound. I imagine they love each other and are dedicated to loving each other.

Again, whether you choose to stay or leave, please continue to love. Create your own nest where you can love yourself and others. Persist in your love. Love yourself well. Love others well. Love your mate, even if it means from a distance. Maintain healthy boundaries, ensuring safety, so that you can love freely.

The Path Forward

It is time to bring this book to a close. There is so much more I could say, and I will wonder what I've forgotten. Is there a critical concept left unsaid?

I hope you will forgive me if I have not spoken strongly enough about a particular issue. I hope you will understand I am writing about something not fully understood.

The path you are on is a relatively new one. Many have gone before you, but the path of recovery from narcissistic and emotional abuse is still newly formed. You are a trailblazer in every sense of the word.

I hope you will let your voice be known. Teach friends, family, churches, and communities about narcissistic and emotional abuse. Teach the teachers. Teach the counselors who think they know what they're talking about, but are naive—including me.

I wish you God's best in your path forward.

Notes

Chapter 1: Swept Off Your Feet

1. *Diagnostic and Statistical Manual of Mental Disorders*, 4th ed. (Washington, DC: American Psychiatric Association, 1994).

Chapter 2: Power, Privilege, and Personality

1. Mike Bundrant, "10 Traits of Powerful People," PsychCentral, September 7, 2015, http://blogs.psychcentral.com/power-submission/2015/09/10-traits-of-powerful-people/.
2. Mary Lamia, "Envy: The Emotion Kept Secret," Psychology Today, March 15, 2011, https://www.psychologytoday.com/blog/intense-emotions-and-strong-feelings/201103/envy-the-emotion-kept-secret.
3. Tomas Chamorro-Premuzic, "The Dark Side of Charisma," *Harvard Business Review*, November 16, 2012, https://hbr.org/2012/11/the-dark-side-of-charisma.
4. Mark Banschick, "The Dangerous Attraction of Powerful Men," Psychology Today, September 18, 2013, https://www.psychologytoday.com/blog/the-intelligent-divorce/201309/the-dangerous-attraction-powerful-men.

Chapter 3: Falling for Him Again

1. Lundy Bancroft, *Why Does He Do That?* (New York: Berkley Books, 2003), 98.
2. Robert Weiss, "This Is Your Brain on Love," *Psychology Today*, January 28, 2015, https://www.psychologytoday.com/blog/love-and-sex-in-the-digital-age/201501/is-your-brain-love.
3. Ibid.
4. Ibid.
5. Scott Peck, *The Road Less Traveled* (New York: Simon & Schuster, 1978), 88-89.
6. Ibid., 89.
7. Brittany Wong, "9 Signs You're in Love with a Narcissist," *Huffington Post*, March 30, 2015, http://www.huffingtonpost.com/2015/03/30/sorry-youre-in-love-with-a-narcissist-_n_6956408.html.

Chapter 4: How Dare You Say That!

1. Dr. John M. Gohol, "15 Common Cognitive Distortions," *PsychCentral*, https://psychcentral.com/lib/15-common-cognitive-distortions/.
2. Kathleen Krajco, "Narcissists Hypersensitive? To What?" *What Makes Narcissists Tick?* (blog), February 5, 2007, http://narc-attack.blogspot.com/2007/02/narcissists-hypersensitive-to-what.html.
3. Sam Vaknin, *Malignant Self Love: Narcissism Revisited* (Czech Republic: Narcissus Publications, 2015). http://www.escapeabuse.com/MSL8.htm.
4. Aubyn De Lisle, "The Wounded Self—The Torture of Narcissism," Counselling Directory, January 22, 2015, http://www.counselling-directory.org.uk/counsellor-articles/the-wounded-self-the-torture-of-narcissism.

5. Craig Malkin,"5 Early Warning Signs You're with a Narcissist," *Psychology Today*, June 21, 2013, https://www.psychologytoday.com/blog/romance-redux/201306/5-early-warning-signs-youre-narcissist.
6. Michael J. Formica, "Understanding the Dynamics of Abusive Relationships," *Psychology Today*, July 14, 2008, https://www.psychologytoday.com/blog/enlightened-living/200807/understanding-the-dynamics-abusive-relationships.
7. Ibid.

Chapter 5: Narcissistic Victim Syndrome

1. Christine Hammond, "Identifying Victims of Narcissistic Abuse," *PsychCentral*, October 13, 2015, https://pro.psychcentral.com/exhausted-woman/2015/10/identifying-victims-of-narcissistic-abuse/.
2. Marylene Cloitre et al., "Distinguishing PTSD, Complex PTSD, and Borderline Personality Disorder: A latent class analysis," *European Journal of Psycho-Traumatology*, September 15, 2014, http://www.tandfonline.com/doi/full/10.3402/ejpt.v5.25097.
3. Kim Saeed, "6 Strong Signs You Have Narcissistic Abuse Syndrome," *Let Me Reach*, October 12, 2015,https://letmereach.com/2015/10/12/6-strong-signs-you-have-narcissistic-abuse-syndrome/.
4. Lundy Bancroft, *Why Does He Do That?* (New York: Berkley Publishing Group, 2002), 98.

Chapter 6: The Many Faces of Emotional Abuse

1. Mary J. Yerkes, "FAQs About Emotional Abuse," *Focus on the Family*, 2007, http://www.focusonthefamily.com/lifechallenges/abuse-and-addiction/understanding-emotional-abuse/faqs-about-emotional-abuse.
2. Lisa Arends, "Subtle Signs You're Being Manipulated by a Covert Abuser," *Lessons from the End of a Marriage*, October 13, 2015, https://lessonsfromtheendofamarriage.com/2015/10/13/subtle-signs-youre-being-manipulated-by-a-covert-abuser/.
3. Abby Rodman, "You're Not Going Crazy: 5 Sure Signs You're Being Emotionally Abused," *Huffington Post*, December 29, 2015, http://www.huffingtonpost.com/abby-rodman-licsw/youre-not-going-crazy-5-s_b_8889808.html.

Chapter 7: Enabling as Secondary Abuse

1. Mira Kirshenbaum, *I Love You, But I Don't Trust You* (New York: Berkley Books, 2012), 211-12.
2. Dr. George Jantz, "Have We Learned to Ignore Emotional Abuse?" *Psychology Today*, May 3, 2016, https://www.psychologytoday.com/blog/hope-relationships/201605/have-we-learned-ignore-emotional-abuse.
3. Candace Love, *No More Narcissists* (Oakland, CA: New Harbinger Publications, 2016), 32.
4. Ibid., 165.
5. Lundy Bancroft, *Should I Stay or Should I Go?* (New York: Berkley Books, 2011), 98.
6. Ibid., 252.
7. Ibid., 208.
8. Patricia Evans, *The Verbally Abusive Relationship* (Avon, MA: Adams Media, 2010), 198-99.
9. Ibid., 210.

Chapter 8: When the Church Is Abusive

1. Paul Hegstrom, *Angry Men and the Women Who Love Them: Breaking the Cycle of Physical and Emotional Abuse* (Kansas City: Beacon Hill Press, 2004), cited in Mary Yerkes, "Emotional Abuse in the Local Church," *Focus on the Family*, http://www.focusonthefamily.com/lifechallenges/abuse-and-addiction/understanding-emotional-abuse/emotional-abuse-in-the-local-church.
2. Rachel Held Evans, "Patriarchy and Abusive Churches," Rachel Held Evans, March 14, 2014, https://rachelheldevans.com/blog/patriarchy-abuse.
3. Hegstrom, *Angry Men and the Women Who Love Them.*
4. Will van der Hart, "Words Matter—Emotional Abuse and the Church," *Mind and Soul,* September 29, 2014, http://www.mindandsoul.info/Articles/416673/Mind_and_Soul/Resources/Words_Matter_Emotional.aspx.

Chapter 9: Growing Smaller and Smaller

1. Martha Brockenbrough, "Is Your Partner Emotionally Abusive?" *Women's Health Magazine*, January 26, 2010, http://www.womenshealthmag.com/sex-and-love/emotional-abuse.
2. Andrea Schneider, "Unreality Check: Cognitive Dissonance in Narcissistic Abuse," *Good Therapy*, October 7, 2014, http://www.goodtherapy.org/blog/unreality-check-cognitive-dissonance-in-narcissistic-abuse-1007144.
3. Ibid.
4. Kellie Jo Holly, "CrazyMaking: Domestic Abuse Intended to Cause Self-Doubt," *Verbal Abuse Journals*, http://verbalabusejournals.com/about-abuse/crazymaking/.
5. Cited in Sarah Klein, "9 Things Your Brain Fog is Trying To Tell You," *Prevention*, July 31, 2015, http://www.prevention.com/health/brain-fog-and-your-health.
6. Dr. Steven Stosny, "Emotional Abuse (Overcoming Victim Identity)," *Psychology Today*, November 18, 2008, https://www.psychologytoday.com/blog/anger-in-the-age-entitlement/200811/emotional-abuse-overcoming-victim-identity.

Chapter 10: Change Begins with You

1. Marc Perry, "Five Stages of Change Model: Which Stage Are You In?" *Built Lean,* October 14, 2016, http://www.builtlean.com/2010/06/01/5-stages-of-change-model-which-stage-are-you-in/.

Chapter 11: The Truth Will Set You Free

1. Aubrey Sampson, "The Most Dangerous Lies Women Believe," *Today's Christian Woman,* November 11, 2015, http://www.todayschristianwoman.com/articles/2015/november-11/shame-you-are-not-enough.html.
2. Ibid.
3. Winn Collier, "Do You Want to Be Whole?" *In Touch Ministries*, January 15, 2015, https://www.intouch.org/read/magazine/features/do-you-want-to-be-whole.
4. Brian Grazer, *A Curious Mind* (New York: Simon & Schuster, 2015), 7.
5. Julia Cameron, *The Artist's Way* (New York: Jeremy P. Tarcher, 1992), 53-54.
6. Scott Peck, *The Road Less Traveled* (New York: Simon & Schuster, 1978), 15.

Chapter 12: Maintaining Dignity with Boundaries

1. Fred Hoyle, *The Intelligent Universe* (New York: Michael Joseph, 1983), 19.
2. Henry Cloud and John Townsend, *Boundaries: When to Say Yes, How to Say No to Take Control of Your Life* (Grand Rapids, MI: Zondervan, 1992), 33.
3. Donald Miller, *Scary Close* (Nashville, TN: Thomas Nelson, 2014), 206-7.
4. Kellie Jo Holly, "Personal Boundaries Are Important for Abuse Victims," *Verbal Abuse Journals*, http://verbalabusejournals.com/how-stop-abuse/setting-personal-boundaries/.
5. Joyce Meyer, *Approval Addiction* (New York: Warner Faith, 2005), 207.
6. William Bridges, *The Way of Transition* (Cambridge, MA: Perseus, 2001), 53.
7. Ibid., 58.
8. Robin Norwood, *Women Who Love Too Much* (New York: Pocket Books, 1985), 261.
9. Lundy Bancroft, *Should I Stay or Should I Go?* (New York: Berkeley Books, 2011), 257.
10. Ibid., 266-68.
11. Jordan and Margaret Paul, *Do I Have to Give Up Me to Be Loved by You?* (New York: MJF Books, 1983), 115.

Chapter 13: Rediscovering Your Godly Self

1. Brian Morton, "Falser Words Were Never Spoken," *New York Times*, August 29, 2011, http://www.nytimes.com/2011/08/30/opinion/falser-words-were-never-spoken.html.
2. Henrik Edberg, "Gandhi's 10 Rules for Changing the World," *Daily Good*, June 28, 2013, http://www.dailygood.org/story/466/gandhi-s-10-rules-for-changing-the-world-henrik-edberg/.
3. Mysia Anderson, "Self-Care Is Resistance," *The Stanford Daily*, May 21, 2015, http://www.stanforddaily.com/2015/05/21/self-care-is-resistance/.
4. Viktor Frankl, *Man's Search for Meaning* (New York: Beacon Press, 1959).
5. Stephen R. Covey, *The 8th Habit* (New York: Free Press, 2004), 5, 40.
6. Henry Cloud and John Townsend, *Safe People* (Grand Rapids, MI: Zondervan, 1995), 29.

About the Author

Dr. David Hawkins is a Christian clinical psychologist, a best-selling author, and the director of the Marriage Recovery Center. With more than 30 years of experience counseling individuals and couples, Dr. Hawkins has become a leading expert on narcissistic and emotional abuse, and a voice of hope for those longing for healing. He and his team of counselors have helped thousands of individuals and couples find lasting freedom from narcissistic and emotional abuse through his unique approach and curriculum.

The Marriage Recovery Center offers a comprehensive program for men struggling in these areas, including a four-day men's small-group intensive, weekly online group intensives, and individualized personal intensives for men. Dr. Hawkins' team also leads four-day women's intensives and offers a subscription group called Thrive, both designed to help women heal from narcissistic and emotional abuse.

Dr. Hawkins is a speaker for the American Association of Christian Counselors and writes regularly for *Crosswalk.com*, *CBN.org*, and *Believe.com*. He has also been featured on *Focus on the Family*, *The 700 Club*, *Time for Hope*, the Trinity Broadcasting Network, and Moody Bible Radio. Dr. Hawkins is happily married to Christie and lives on Bainbridge Island near Seattle.

Learn more about Dr. Hawkins and the Marriage Recovery Center at **www.marriagerecoverycenter.com.**

Also by Dr. David Hawkins...

When Pleasing Others Is Hurting You

You want to do the right thing—to take care of your family, to be a good employee, to "be there" for your friends. And you're good at it. Everyone knows they can depend on you—so they do.

But are you really doing what's best for them? And what about you—are you growing? Are you happy and relaxed? Are you excited about your gifts and your calling, or do you sometimes think,

"I don't even know what I want anymore."

Find out why you have trouble saying no. Learn why you feel accepted only when you are producing. And finally experience the deep joy and peace that come with serving other people out of your abundance, not out of your need.